Captain Fitz

Captain Fitz

FitzGibbon, Green Tiger of the War of 1812

Enid Mallory

DUNDURN
TORONTO

Editor: Cheryl Hawley
Design: Courtney Horner
Printer: Marquis

Library and Archives Canada Cataloguing in Publication

Mallory, Enid, 1938-
    Captain Fitz : FitzGibbon, Green Tiger of the War
of 1812 / by Enid Mallory.

Includes bibliographical references and index.
Issued also in electronic formats.
ISBN 978-1-4597-0118-2

    1. FitzGibbon, James, 1780-1863. 2. Canada--History--War of
1812. 3. Soldiers--Canada--Biography. I. Title.

FC443.F58M34 2011   971.03'4092   C2011-903859-5

1   2   3   4   5   15   14   13   12   11

We acknowledge the support of the **Canada Council for the Arts** and the **Ontario Arts Council** for our publishing program. We also acknowledge the financial support of the **Government of Canada** through the **Canada Book Fund** and **Livres Canada Books**, and the **Government of Ontario** through the **Ontario Book Publishing Tax Credit** and the **Ontario Media Development Corporation.**

Care has been taken to trace the ownership of copyright material used in this book. The author and the publisher welcome any information enabling them to rectify any references or credits in subsequent editions.

J. Kirk Howard, President

Printed and bound in Canada.
www.dundurn.com

Dundurn
3 Church Street, Suite 500
Toronto, Ontario, Canada
M5E 1M2

Gazelle Book Services Limited
White Cross Mills
High Town, Lancaster, England
LA1 4XS

Dundurn
2250 Military Road
Tonawanda, NY
U.S.A. 14150

For young historians on both sides
of the world's longest undefended border

CONTENTS

INTRODUCTION

Captain Fitz is the story of a young Irishman, James FitzGibbon, who became a British soldier, an unlikely event, as the Irish mistrusted the English and the British Army did not accept Irish Catholics until 1799. Fitz was able to join in 1798, because his family had turned Protestant.

By 1812, he was a lieutenant, and in 1813 he was promoted to captain. In 1826, Fitz became colonel of the West York Militia Regiment of Canada.

For a poor Irish boy, the British Army was no easy road to success. To make it, he needed determination, skill, intelligence, and boundless energy, all of which he had. He would also need to educate himself — with the help of Isaac Brock, he did.

While this is a book about the War of 1812, it does not seek to glorify war but to understand it, to see how it shaped Canada, and consider how future generations can prevent it.

Fifty years after the war, historian James Croil wrote about the animosity that remained on both sides of the border. He calls the war "… an unnatural and aggressive demonstration … destined by Providence to teach future ages the folly of rushing unprovoked and unprepared into hostilities, that might easily and honourably be settled by diplomatic negotations."[1]

As a "Green Tiger," Captain Fitz fought in the War of 1812 with all the ferocity of a tiger, dedicated to the British cause, intent on winning, and seeking the fame and glory that came with success. But he understood that the American soldiers, caught up in a war declared by an aggressive president, often shared common bonds with the British and Canadian men they fought.

Once peace was achieved, FitzGibbon worked tirelessly to maintain it. In 1824, he was sent to Perth, where riots had broken out between Irish Catholic and Protestant settlers. He spent three weeks talking to both sides, often in the Gaelic tongue, hearing their problems and quieting conflicts. Near Peterborough, when there was trouble again between Protestants and Catholics, he played a similar role. He also wrote letters to Orange Lodges (Protestant organizations), urging restraint and suggesting that they not march in their Orange parades.

In 1837, when William Lyon Mackenzie's rebels marched on Toronto, FitzGibbon's awareness and military organization is credited with saving the city and possibly the province.

He understood the horrors of war. As he stood remembering Isaac Brock at the dedication of his monument in 1824, Fitz felt a great loneliness, almost all of his 49th Regiment had been killed in the War of 1812.

Fitz survived the battles and the predicaments he got himself into and lived to be 83 years old.

CHAPTER 1
AN IRISH LAD

Colonel F. is a soldier of fortune — which phrase means, in his case at least, that he owes nothing whatever to fortune, but everything to his own good heart, his own good sense, and his own good sword. He was the son, and glories in it, of an Irish cotter, on the estate of the Knight of Glyn.
— Anna Jameson, *Winter Studies and Summer Rambles in Canada, 1838*[1]

In the midsummer heat of 1812, at Lachine on the St. Lawrence River, a young lieutenant is struggling to organize 24 boatloads of soldiers and army provisions to embark for Kingston. He's excited and satisfied with himself. After 10 years in the Canadas, he has been made a lieutenant in the 49th Regiment under Sir Isaac Brock. He has a war, a command, a devotion to all things British, and a land he deems worth fighting for.

James FitzGibbon (Fitz to his friends) was born in a cottage on the River Shannon in Ireland. He grew up with a love of adventure, curious about the bigger world. His interest in far-away places and times made him read every book he could get his hands on. His family only owned one book, *The History of Troy's Destruction*. He was too little to understand most of the words but he kept it hidden in his cot and "read it to pieces," grasping more of it each time. He became known as the best reader in the school, and when other boys had money for a

FitzGibbon in the 49th Regiment wore a red tunic with green cuffs and facings. Here Stoney Creek enactors wear the uniforms of the 49th.

Enid Mallory.

book they would ask James to choose for them. He always chose one he hadn't read so he could borrow and read it later.

James was a determined kid and quick as a cat. He was eight years old the day he dragged the big salmon home. Its length was more than he could lift from the ground. He had spied it in the brook by the old castle and leaped in after it, dragged it up the bank, and gaffed it with a rusty old knife.

He was 15 when his father enrolled himself, his eldest son, and James in the yeomanry corps being formed to defend Ireland against threatened invasion by France. Life changed then for the boys, brought up in a Catholic village where the words Protestant and English had usually been words of hate. His father, Garrett, had probably turned Protestant because it enabled him to own his own land (no Catholic could). Since the FitzGibbons were the only Protestant family in the village, their home was an obvious choice when British soldiers, sent in response to a threatened French invasion, needed lodging. It was a great surprise to James that the Protestant English soldiers billeted in his home were likable, fun-loving human beings. In the evenings, the soldiers would drill the older FitzGibbon boys in the kitchen, and laugh and play with the younger ones. Old prejudices fell away and horizons expanded for James.

One day, when the corporal who had drilled their corps was suddenly ordered to join his regiment, the captain, newly returned from England and unfamiliar with the new system of drilling, attempted to put the men through their exercises. The ignorance and confusion of the corps drove the captain into a white-hot rage. While the older men stood speechless, young James stepped out and said, "The men are not to blame, sir. You are giving us words of command we have never heard."[2] Then he stood there quaking, expecting the captain's wrath on his head.

Instead, after a pause of astonishment, the captain asked James to put the men through their exercises. The men did well and James was asked to go on drilling them. A few days later he found a sergeant's pike, sword, and sash sent to his house with an order appointing James FitzGibbon to sergeant over men much older than himself, his father and brother included.

In 1798, when Fitz was 17, the first lieutenant of the corps had been given a company in the new Tarbert Fencibles and had persuaded James to join as pay-sergeant. He was delighted to hear that they would be going to England.

His mother was not happy. She moved with unaccustomed slowness as she helped him pack. What would an Irish boy be doing in the British Army? Without money or friends in high places, he had little hope of obtaining a commission. She made him promise that he would never enlist for active service abroad. Just before he fell asleep that night, he heard her extracting the same promise from his captain. He had no intention of volunteering for active service. Going to England would be adventure enough.

That promise held him for while. But in 1799, at the age of 18, James left the Tarbert Fencibles and was drafted into the 49th Regiment as sergeant. He said afterward that he never intended to do it, but the persuasion of a recruiting general and the pressure of 40 men who said that would volunteer only if FitzGibbon did, along with his natural zest for adventure, had blotted out the promise to his mother.

When Mrs. FitzGibbon read the letter that James sent to tell her about the commission, she shuddered. The odds were that he would remain a sergeant, subject to all the hardship, terrible danger, and possible degradation inherent in the army system. Then she remembered his remarkable faculty for landing on his feet in whatever situation. Maybe …

The morning after his enlistment he sailed for the invasion of Holland, which landed him briefly in a French prison and erased his misconceptions about the glories of war. Two years later, when he was 20, he sailed under Lord Nelson against Denmark. Then, in June 1802, the 49th was sent to the Canadas to be stationed at Quebec.

During the previous three years, Fitz had served under Isaac Brock, a commander who was already Fitz's personal hero and who was destined to become the hero of Upper Canada. Brock, lieutenant-colonel of the 49th Regiment, combined all the best qualities of a British officer, qualities James and his mother had not dared hope to find in an army that was notorious for high-nosed arrogance, tyrannical discipline, and outright brutality. Isaac Brock tempered strict discipline with kindness, fairness, and faith in his men; and he gave them an example of personal courage, good humour, and pride. Under Brock, the 49th earned the nickname of "Green Tigers," a title that aptly described their daring, as well as the green facings on their jackets.

"Out of one of the worst regiments in the service," the Duke of York reported, "Colonel Brock has made the 49th one of the best." Out of the young impulsive boy from Ireland, Colonel Brock was making an outstanding soldier who would dare anything for his commander and for the British cause.

Brock had been quick to see the promise in young FitzGibbon. He had noticed that the Irish lad was scrupulously honest and his standard of honour so high that when he was reprimanded by Colonel Hutchinson, he asked to resign as sergeant and be demoted to private. When Brock heard of this he suggested a simple apology to Hutchinson and reinstated him as sergeant. He was further surprised when FitzGibbon spoke up suggesting it was wrong for an officer to scold a non-commissioned officer in front of his men, because it was detrimental to discipline.

On the long voyage to Quebec, Brock often smiled at the sight of James propped up in one of the swaying lifeboats, surrounded by books of military tactics and field exercises. Isaac suspected the young Fitz must have memorized the entire *Rules and Regulations for the Field Exercises of His Majesty's Forces* by the time they sighted land. On arrival at Quebec, Brock promoted James to sergeant-major of the regiment over 40 older sergeants, and made James his staff-sergeant.

The Canadas, Upper and Lower, were governed from London, with capitals at Quebec in Lower Canada and at York (Toronto) in Upper Canada. A governor-in-chief was stationed at Quebec and a lieutenant-governor at York. Although Europe was in turmoil because of the Napoleonic wars, the Canadas from 1802 to 1810 were mainly peaceful, affording no great adventure or opportunity for advancement. England had neither time nor troops to spare for a war in America, so those who governed and those who commanded in the Canadas were cautioned to keep a careful and watchful peace with neighbours to the south.

Canadian Countryside 1802–12

Quebec and Montreal were lively towns in 1802 and the farms of 60,000 Canadiens were laid out along the river. But as one moved upcountry, forest pressed hard against the shore, broken only by a few cabins along the front or by a mill site where grain could be ground or lumber sawn. Loyalists, fleeing persecution after the American Revolution, had been here for only two decades. In the early-settled townships of Dundas, Stormont, and Glengarry, some of the log cabins were being replaced by stout stone houses crafted by Scottish or German masons who had served in the Kings Royal Rangers under Sir John Johnson.

Along with the Loyalists, there were later arrivals from the United States, attracted by cheap land. It was Governor Simcoe's desire to increase settlement along the frontier to strengthen the country. Most of these settlers would become good Canadians, but a few could not be counted on in time of trouble.

Upper Canada's first road was cut through the bush close to the river, from Cornwall to Kingston. Passable on winter snow, it became a quagmire in spring and a bone-rattling ride in summer. Walking was the quickest way to get somewhere by land, but as soon as the St. Lawrence River and the lakes were free of ice, travel was by boat.

A second road existed as early as 1795, a portage around Niagara Falls from Queenston to Chippawa. As many as 50 wagons a day in summer and ox-sleds in winter carried furs downstream and merchandise upstream from Quebec.

The Danforth Road was started in 1798 from the Bay of Quinte to Bath, through Prince Edward County to the Carrying Place, then along Lake Ontario to York. By 1800, it was open from Kingston to Ancaster, but in bad repair. In many areas, the lakeshore itself was the only road. Many of the missing links would not be opened until after the War of 1812.

Kingston, where Fort Frontenac had overlooked Lake Ontario since 1673, would play a major role as the shipbuilding centre in this war. Farther west, York, which had a good harbour at the mouth of two rivers, had been made the capital of Upper Canada by Governor Simcoe in 1796. The barracks, blockhouse, and powder magazine were three kilometres west of the town, beside Government House. The elite light company of the 49th was stationed here as well as the 41st Foot.

Because many Loyalists entered Upper Canada at Niagara, settlement there was advanced. Settlers found a fertile land and a climate moderated by the escarpment and the lake and had well-established farms by 1812. Unfortunately, they were centre stage for much of the fiercest fighting in the coming war.

Edwin Guillet, *Pioneer Travel*, 139 (Coke Smyth, 1838).

The St. Lawrence River was Canada's best highway in 1812, whether open for boats and canoes or frozen in winter.

During these years, FitzGibbon was Brock's faithful sergeant-major; whenever the colonel faced trouble, Fitz was there. In 1803, at York, when three soldiers took a military bateau and deserted across Lake Ontario, Brock took James and 10 other men and set out at midnight to row across Lake Ontario and capture them.

That same year, when news reached York that mutiny had broken out at Niagara's Fort George against the tyrannical authority of General Sheaffe, Fitz was the man chosen to accompany Brock to deal with the problem. Sheaffe was the kind of officer James's mother had dreaded when he joined the British Army, quick to administer the lash for the most trifling of offences. At Fort George the men had had all they could take and they were striking back out of desperation. But discipline had to be restored.

Brock walked into the fort and, by sheer force of personality, made one of the ringleaders lay down his arms and another one handcuff him. Brock then had the drummer arouse the garrison and within a half hour had 11 mutineers handcuffed and on board the schooner for York. James was sent with the prisoners to Quebec, where their trial took place and the leaders were executed by firing squad.

During those years, Brock kept Fitz supplied with books and taught him not only the arts of the military but the manners and lifestyle of a gentleman. Brock also taught Fitz to go about doing the impossible. Only once did FitzGibbon tell Brock that something was impossible. "By the Lord Harry, sir, do not tell me it is impossible," thundered Brock. "Nothing should be impossible to a soldier. The word impossible should not be found in a soldier's dictionary."[3]

James never forgot that. In 1807, when there was fear of American invasion, Brock ordered James to bring him 20 bateaux to embark troops for Montreal. FitzGibbon found the boats left high by the tide, separated by 180 metres of mud from the water to float them. It would be impossible to move them. He had turned his men away when his imagination heard a familiar voice asking, "Did you try it, sir?"

"Front!" he ordered his men. "I think it impossible for us to put these bateaux afloat, but you know it will not do to tell the colonel so, unless we try it. Let us

Protegé of Isaac Brock

It was not easy for a young Irish lad with poor schooling and no money to advance in an army where British sons of nobility purchased their officers' commissions. Fitz was helped up the slippery military ladder first of all by his intelligence, devotion to duty, and strength and agility of body and mind; and second by Isaac Brock, who noticed his initiative and made him his protegé. In a letter to Brock's nephew, Ferdinand Brock Tupper, Fitz recalled how Brock plied him with books and encouraged him to educate himself. He told a story of taking dictation from Brock in Montreal in 1802. "I then did not know the difference between a verb and a noun!" The last word Brock dictated was ascertain, *which Fitz pronounced "ascerten." Brock, pacing back and forth, turned and said, "Ascertain, young man!"*

> *At that time my ignorance of my real deficiencies was very great, and I thought myself quite sufficient master of the language. But this discovery of one error roused me, and I went into Town the same day and bought a Grammar and a Dictionary, Books which I had never even seen before, and on studying them I was amazed at my great ignorance of every thing which the Grammar taught."[4]*

There were other lessons to learn. Isaac Brock deplored corporal punishment, the mainstay of British Army discipline. Fitz observed that the authority of Brock over his men was based on kindness, in contrast to Major-General Sheaffe, Brock's second-in-command in the 49th Regiment who seemed to delight in cruelty.

Examples from the Returns of the 49th Regiment show the extremes of punishment by the lash: "Deficient of frill, part of his regimental necessaries. Sentenced 100; inflicted. For being deficient of a shirt, part of his regimental necessaries. Sentenced 200; inflicted 75. Drunk before morning parade although confined to barracks. Sentenced 200; 150 inflicted."

When possible, Brock commuted the sentence by half. Some of the soldiers were rough, ignorant men with criminal backgrounds, but he never forgot they were human beings. FitzGibbon, who also deplored corporal punishment, watched and learned from Brock how to discipline men without cruelty and how to inspire loyalty.

try — there are the boats. I am sure if it is possible for men to put them afloat, you will do it; go at them." In half an hour it was done.

For the next five years the small British garrison in the Canadas kept an uneasy eye on the border with United States. By 1812, the threatened invasion from the south was becoming a reality.

Naval blockades arising from Napoleon's Berlin Decree and Britain's answering orders-in-council had ended the peace. Britain's was searching neutral ships for deserters, which infuriated many Americans. Although the northern states did not want war against the Canadas, the war party in Congress, prodded by western states hungry to usurp Native lands and claiming the British were supporting Native uprisings, proved too strong for the moderates.

By the spring of 1812 you could taste war all along the frontier. To James FitzGibbon, it was a tangy, exciting taste — here was his long-awaited opportunity for advancement. He resigned the adjutancy of the 49th Regiment and was made a lieutenant in command of a company.

CHAPTER 2
WAR WITH AMERICA

Sir George Prevost desires me to inform you that he has this instant received intelligence from Mr. Richardson by an express to the Northwest Company, announcing that the American Government had declared war against Great Britain.

— Colonel Baynes to Major-General Brock, June 25, 1812[1]

The brigade of bateaux loaded with soldiers moved slowly into the St. Lawrence River from Lachine. Lieutenant James FitzGibbon filled his lungs with the clean river air. He was delighted to be moving upcountry now that war with the United States was declared. Since his arrival in Quebec, 10 years before, he had travelled this river often and knew it in any mood. He had an uncanny instinct for geography and knew the shoreline from Quebec to Niagara with an accuracy that surprised even Natives and those fur-trader explorers called *Voyageurs*, who used rivers and lakes to push far inland and send furs home to England.

FitzGibbon also had a good sense of history — after all, at eight years old he had read *The History of Troy's Destruction*. He felt the ghosts of the past moving on this river: Mohawks going west to fight Huron or Ojibway tribes; Champlain pushing into the interior; General Wolfe sailing up to Quebec to meet Montcalm on the Plains of Abraham; North West Company explorers; Loyalists crossing the

Guillet, 34 (F. Levin).

This flat-bottomed bateau, being loaded with provisions, would be sailed, rowed, poled, and dragged upstream from Montreal to Kingston.

river after the American Revolution so they could live under the British flag. He knew this river would once again become a highway of war.

He might, of course, be killed fighting this war. But until then, he would have action, excitement, possibly promotion. In the British Army, visions of honour and glory were the motivating forces. Promotion could pave the way. Every officer was ready to die for his country's cause, as long as he could do it gloriously.

Fitz had a heavy job getting 24 boatloads of soldiers, arms, ammunition, and provisions up this wild river. The bateaux were 9 to 13 metres long and over a metre-and-a-half wide. The sides rose straight up to a height of 1.2 metres; the sharply pointed bow and stern came up 30 centimetres higher. White oak formed the bottom, light fir the sides. These remarkably adaptable boats could be rowed, poled, and sailed, and they almost never capsized. Best of all, they were flat-bottomed and could slide over the great boulders of the Cedars and Long Sault Rapids.

On Lac-St.-Louis, the French-Canadian boatmen hoisted their lug sails and the boats sailed before a rare, light east wind. Without a keel and a weather helm, and with crude rigging, bateaux could only sail well before the wind, which usually blew from the west.

Ahead lay the Cascades, the Cedars, and the Coteau Rapids. The attention of the entire brigade was fastened on the scene before them, as a bateaux and a larger Durham boat came flying down the Cedars and Cascades. These shallow rapids were considered the most dangerous on the St. Lawrence. The two craft, caught up in the furious, churning, white madness, seemed to leap and plunge in the maelstrom. In one place, as James knew well, the long downhill plunge was like a mill race. But he and his soldiers heard the triumphant cries of *"Vive Le Roi"* as the boats rose out of that run, and his soldiers and boatmen answered with their own cheers of congratulation. It was a drama re-enacted daily, but not always happily — as burial crosses on the shoreline testified.

FitzGibbon and crew, bound upriver, had a few small locks to help them over the worst places. The first had been cut through limestone at Coteau-du-Lac in 1781. A few more had been crudely constructed to help the Loyalists move upriver, and in 1804 some of the locks had been improved and enlarged by the Royal

Descending the Cascade Rapids was always exciting, sometimes tragic.

Guillet, 34 (George Heriot).

Engineers. But for hour after hour, poling and tracking were the order of the hot summer days. With the soldiers disembarked, the crew would thrust iron-tipped poles into the channel and work their way up the rocks, or the crewmen would jump into the water, often up to their armpits, and, with loops over their shoulders, haul or track the boats against the current while one oarsman remained on board, steering with a long sweep. When rough terrain made tracking impossible, boats had to be dragged over skidways made of logs.

The 40 kilometres of Lac St.-François provided calm water again. At night, FitzGibbon's soldiers and crewmen bivouacked on the shore, but they pressed on again by the early light of midsummer dawn. From the Native village of St. Regis at the foot of the 14.5-kilometre Long Sault Rapids, FitzGibbon kept his brigade against the south shore. This American shoreline was enemy territory where they might be ambushed at any time, but it also provided the easiest, swiftest route through the rapids, the one that his boatmen knew best. Time was important and risk was inevitable in time of war.

The river remains narrow and swift above the Long Sault, with small villages on either shore. By 1812, the south shore was more bustling and built-up than the north, but even on the Canadian shore the heavy forest was broken by a few well-kept farms, like Crysler's above the Long Sault; the Loyalists' huts were being replaced by stout stone houses and small villages like Matilda (Iroquois) and Prescott. There was tension as they passed Prescott, for the St. Lawrence runs narrow there and raids were expected. Above Prescott they could lose themselves in the islands and the soldiers could relax and brag about what they'd do to 'em at Kingston or York or Fort Erie if the Americans came a callin'.

FitzGibbon's nimble mind catalogued the countryside, the pretty town just passed on the right, established by Augusta Jones (later to be called Brockville), the pitch pine trees on the island, the flight of wild ducks, herons, kingfishers, a bald eagle once. But another part of his mind staged battles, pondered methods of attack, ambush, surprise! Surprise would be important in small battles. He envisioned a war that would be different from the war he had seen briefly in Europe. It might even be different from anything his senior officers expected or could

St. Lawrence Supply Route

Canada's great river flows from Lake Ontario, 1,197 kilometres to the sea. Some even say it begins in the headwaters of Lake Superior, almost 2,000 kilometres to the west. Navigable from the sea to Montreal, explorers found it an open invitation to the interior of a vast continent. From Montreal to Prescott they found it less inviting, as they had to struggle against the rapids of Lachine and Long Sault. For the next 320 kilometres, ships were replaced by flat-bottomed bateaux, which could be rowed or poled or towed up the rapids, then sailed where the river was calm.

Above Prescott, the river becomes complacent and scenic as it spreads among the Thousand Islands. At the east end of Lake Ontario, a traveller in 1812 would come to Kingston's naval yards and could embark on a ship again.

This was the supply route on which the British Army depended to move all military and naval stores — canvas, rope, cables, anchors, guns and shot, as well as troops. The bateaux trip from Montreal to Kingston could take several weeks. Narrow parts of the river — less than a mile wide at Prescott — exposed the boatmen to gunfire from the American shore.

The bateaux convoys had voyageur guides and militia escorts. Calvary and militia were spaced along the "front" from Coteau-du-Lac to Kingston. Militiamen were also farmers who had to sow and reap as well as soldier, and were often not found where the action was.

Sporadic raids kept the bateaux brigades on the alert and caused Governor Sir George Prevost to build Fort Wellington at Prescott and station two companies of the Glengarry Fencibles there. As well, blockhouses were being built at intervals of roughly 80 kilometres to be manned by local militia.

Americans also used the St. Lawrence route along the 160-kilometre river boundary from French Mills near Cornwall to Sackets Harbor opposite Kingston, but, unlike the British, they had an alternate supply route from New York to Oswego via the Hudson and Mohawk rivers, Lake Oneida, and the Syracuse and Oswego rivers.

As the war went on and supplies from the countryside became exhausted, clothing, boots, even flour would have to come from England, pork and beef from Ireland, all costing a fortune by the time they reached the troops at Niagara. But to the delight of British officers, cattle were still being driven from U.S. farms to border crossings in the eastern townships. British officers were happy to pay the Yankee farmers a good price and enjoy the joke.

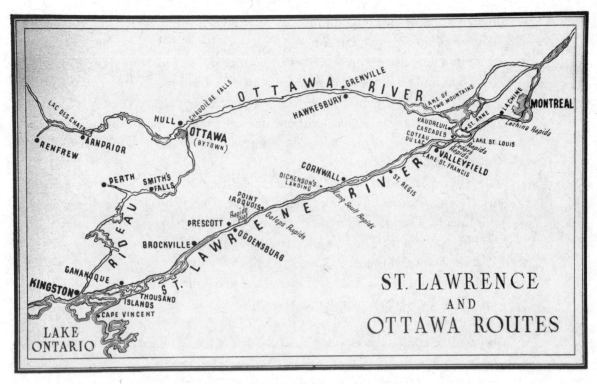

The St. Lawrence River was Canada's 401 Highway in 1812.

handle. Except Brock! Brock would know what he was about. The well-loved colonel of the 49th had become Major-General Isaac Brock, commander of the forces in Upper Canada. In the absence of Lieutenant-Governor Gore, Brock was also appointed administrator of Upper Canada.

Grinning, Fitz recalled the time Brock had thundered at him, "By the Lord Harry, sir, do not tell me it is impossible." As he moved upriver, Fitz was convinced that a full measure of the impossible lay ahead for the gallant major-general. The country was considered lost, not only in the opinion of aggressive Americans but in the minds of most of its inhabitants. England had her hands full in Europe. While she dealt with Napoleon on the high seas and tried to stop his march by land, she could do little to defend what the French had dubbed a "few *arpents* of snow" in North America.

Fitz knew there were only 4,450 regular soldiers in Upper and Lower Canada. The militia amounted to 2,500 men in Lower Canada, 1,800 in Upper Canada. Among the militia there were staunch Loyalists, veterans of the American Revolution who would fight like demons to keep the land British, but most of them were old men; their sons were young and strong, but they were also untried and untrained.

The task ahead of Brock, and officers like himself, was to occupy forts at Kingston, York (Toronto), Newark (Niagara), Chippawa, Fort Erie, Amherstburg, and St. Joseph. They had to escort convoys up the vulnerable St. Lawrence River, as Fitz was doing. They had to defend 1,300 kilometres of frontier in Upper Canada alone. To the Americans, he knew they looked like a handful of redcoat and homespun that would surrender at the first volley. Henry Clay, speaker of the House of Representatives, looking northward with greedy eyes, had declared it "absurd to suppose we shall not succeed." Fitz had also heard that General Porter boasted he could take Upper Canada with a corporal and six men to carry a flag, because the majority of Canada's inhabitants were awaiting the chance to join the United States. President Jefferson had added that it was "a mere matter of marching." Their remarks were not altogether foolish when one considered that British North America had only a half-million settlers against six million Americans, and that a large portion of the population of Upper Canada was of American origin, and not all of them Loyalists.

As Fitz talked with the settlers along the shoreline, in Glengarry and Matilda, and from Prescott to Kingston, he sensed the fear and uncertainty, sometimes even a willingness to be defeated, which enraged him. But occasionally he heard a new note of confidence about having a military administrator of the province. The settlers also seemed to sense something about FitzGibbon, as he moved upriver with his robust soldiers. He was so utterly resolute, so eager. The farmer leaning on his hoe, the woman at her cottage door, felt a little better after he had passed.

Commercial Warfare at Sea

As Napoleon tightened his fist on Europe he sought to weaken England by economic warfare. His Berlin Decree of 1806 forbade French, allied, or neutral ships from trading with England. Britain responded with orders-in-council forbidding vessels to trade with France. Neutral ships were ordered to call at British ports or risk being seized by Britain.

America's trade was hit hard by Britain's blockade as its ships and cargos were seized for violating the embargo. Britain was also boarding American vessels to supposedly search for British Navy deserters. In fact, the boarders were often impressing American citizens into military service. Between 1800 and 1812, an estimated 3,000 to 7,000 Americans were swooped up to serve on British ships.

In June 1807, when the HMS Leopard opened fire on the U.S. frigate Chesapeake and forced the impressment of four crew members, Americans clamoured for war. Jefferson, trying to avoid war, clamped an embargo on U.S. trade, which ruined many ship owners and trading firms.

A final orders-in-council issued in 1811 forbade the U.S. selling of fish to the West Indies. By then the embargos had ruined trade not only in France and America but Britain as well. On June 16, 1812, the orders-in-council were repealed, two days before President Madison declared war. It was too late. News travelled so slowly that word did not reach Madison until 50 days later, on August 12.

Major-General Isaac Brock, as the new administrator of Upper Canada, could combine the military and administrative authority of the country to move quickly when needed. If the impossible had to be done, at least they had the right man in the right place to do it. Fitz could go up the St. Lawrence to Kingston full of confidence.

CHAPTER 3

VICTORY AT DETROIT
AND MACKINAC

We are engaged in an awful and eventful contest. By unanimity and dispatch in our councils, and by vigour in our operation, we may teach the enemy this lesson — that a country defended by free men, enthusiastically devoted to the cause of their king and constitution, can never be conquered!
— Major-General Brock to the Legislature at York, July 28, 1812[1]

As far back as February 1812, Major-General Isaac Brock had written to Governor Sir George Prevost, "Every day hostilities are retarded, the greater the difficulties we shall have to encounter." But war was not officially declared until June 18, and still, on July 28, as he opened a special session of the legislature, Brock did not know whether the Declaration of War had been passed by Congress. He had a war to fight but he could not get at it — at least, he thought he had a war to fight.

Aware that he was unequal to any American show of force (the population of the British colonies was half a million against six to eight million Americans), Brock considered his best weapon to be surprise. If he could move before his enemy was ready he might deal a blow that would greatly inconvenience the Americans, delight the Natives, ally them to the British, and convince the faltering settlers that they could resist the Americans.

His target would be the American Fort Detroit. Detroit and Michilimackinac at the top of Lake Huron were fur-trading posts that controlled the western entrance to Upper Canada. Both had to be in British hands if Brock were to have any hope of holding 1,300 kilometres of frontier with the 1,200 troops he had. On July 12, the American General Hull had arrived at Detroit and crossed the St. Clair River to occupy the Canadian village of Sandwich (today's Windsor).

On July 28, Brock wrote to Governor Sir George Prevost in Quebec, "My situation is getting each day more critical. I still mean to try and send a force to the relief of Amherstburg [the British fort down the St. Clair River from Sandwich], but almost despair of succeeding."[2]

At last, on July 29, Brock received letters from the city of Quebec telling him war was officially declared. Then came the good news that Captain Roberts, stationed at St. Joseph's Island where Lakes Huron and Michigan meet, had collected 180 *Voyageurs* along with his 45 regulars, borrowed boats from the North West Company, and swept down to capture Fort Michilimackinac. Four hundred uncommitted Natives went along to watch. The Americans were so surprised that it never occurred to them to fight. Brock chuckled as he pictured the British flag hoisted over the rocks and trees of that far wilderness.

Then, wonder of wonders, the men of York stirred into action. Brock had just written of them, "A full belief possesses them all that this province must inevitably succumb ... Most of the people have lost all confidence ... I however speak loud and look big." Now here was the York militia volunteering their services to any part of the province. "I have selected 100 whom I have directed to proceed without delay to Long Point, where I propose collecting a force for the relief of Amherstburg,"[3] Brock wrote to Sir George Prevost on July 29.

As Brock made preparations to move toward Detroit, his mind also moved along the St. Lawrence and Niagara frontiers, reviewing the pitifully inadequate means of defence. In the months past he had done what he could with the little he had. A system of convoy, with FitzGibbon bringing the first one, would move regiments and war supplies up the St. Lawrence as soon as they could be spared from Quebec City and Montreal. During the spring they had recruited in Glen-

The York Volunteers

All able-bodied men between 18 and 60 were required to be part of the Sedentary Militia to be called up when needed. They trained about three days a month. The Incorporated Militia, on the other hand, would serve for the entire war. The York Volunteers were an incorporated militia.

The young men who joined it were untried and untrained but they were sons or grandsons of Loyalists, steeped in the lore of war and staunchly anti-American. Most of them had been educated and indoctrinated at Reverend John Strachan's Cornwall school, which by then had moved to York. Brock soon discovered that these young men were a valuable resource.

Five hundred men volunteered for the trek to Amherstburg. Brock chose 250 and added a few more at Niagara and Long Point. Their names read like a list of Who's Who in Upper Canada as many who survive the war go on to fame and fortune. Alexander Hamilton will become sheriff of the Niagara District and member of the legislative council; William Hamilton Merritt will be known as promoter of the Welland Canal; Archibald McLean will become chief justice of the Court of Queen's Bench; George Ridout will align himself with reformers in the House of Assembly, while his brother Thomas becomes first manager of the Bank of Upper Canada; George Ryerson will become a prominent oculist and surgeon; William Allan will become president of the Bank of Upper Canada; Samuel Jarvis, a lawyer, will be famous for the duel in which he killed John Jarvis, while his brother George becomes a judge and member of the House of Assembly. John Beverly Robinson will become attorney general, while his brother Peter will bring 2,500 Irish settlers to found the town of Peterborough.

These are the men around whom the myth about Brock's last words, "Push on, brave York Volunteers!" grew. True or not, it would be reported in the Kingston Gazette *the day following his death. (Most likely, the words were heard by the men marching up the Portage Road as Brock flew past on his horse.) In any case, that slogan would later help to convince many a York volunteer that the militia won the war.*

After the war those names will become synonymous with loyalty to Britain and mistrust of democracy, entrenched power of position, and opposition to reform; they will become the Family Compact. Just now they are young men learning how to fight a war.

garry for a Glengarry Light Infantry Regiment; by May 14, Colonel Baynes could report it complete to 400 rank and file.

An inspecting field officer had moved through the line of settlements to check on the militia and set their quotas. Between Glengarry and Kingston, Brock had urged every man capable of bearing a musket to be prepared to act, and had noted the need for a stronghold in the vicinity of Prescott. FitzGibbon's soldiers waved at carpenters building the new fortification to be known as Fort Wellington. Farmers with heavy teams were drawing timbers and stones for the construction. It cheered the soldiers to know there would be protection if there was a raid from Ogdensburg.

Meanwhile, at York and Niagara, Brock had called out flank companies of militia who would be drilled much like regular soldiers and used in heavy fighting. This produced a force of 800 men, all in need of blankets, haversacks, kettles, and tents. From Fort George he wrote, "The militia assembled in a wretched state in regard to clothing; many were without shoes, an article which can scarcely be provided in

Men of Glengarry

In 1803, Father Alexander McDonell brought Highland Scots to be settled in the eastern corner of Upper Canada. These Irish Catholics were to be a buffer between French Catholics in Lower Canada and the German Protestants who were to be a buffer between them and the English Protestants farther west.

Many of the Scots were soldiers from the disbanded Glengarry Fencible Corp. When war became imminent, these Glengarries were quick to form militia battalions. The Glengarry Light Infantry was raised by the Macdonells. Colonel John Macdonell, a lawyer in York and acting attorney general, became aide-de-camp to Isaac Brock in 1812 and died with him on Queenston Heights. The Glengarry Regiment took part in the defence of York in 1813 and fought the battles at Châteauguay, Crysler's Farm, and Lundy's Lane. This is the regiment that Fitz joined in January 1814, when he was promoted to captain.

the country."[4] These 800 untested soldiers without shoes would have the task of defending the Niagara River line until enough British soldiers could be moved up from Quebec and Kingston. And that depended on regiments being spared from the colossal fight that Britain was engaged in against Napoleon in Europe.

Then there was the question of food. Back in February, Brock had written that he had directed the assistant deputy commissary-general at Amherstburg to purchase 2,000 bushels of Indian corn, "Corn will be absolutely necessary in the event of war." Shrewdly he added, "It is to be procured, if possible, on the American side, that our own stock may remain undiminished."[5]

An American spy, writing to his superiors, expressed envious admiration at Brock's preparation:

> General Brock has paid attention to every particular that can relate to the future resources of the Province. The harvest has been got in tolerably well and greater preparation is making for sowing grain than was ever made before. The militia duty is modified as much as possible to suit the circumstances of the people and measures taken to prevent them from feeling the burden of the war. The women work in the field, encouragement being given for the purpose.[6]

But Brock knew it was not enough. Only a bold stroke could weld British soldier, settler, and Native into a fighting force that would not blow to pieces in the first wind from the south. On August 6, he left York with the York Volunteers for Burlington Bay where they set out overland to Long Point on Lake Erie. There, he picked up the Norfolk Militia under George Ryerson and embarked 260 militia and 40 soldiers of the 41st Regiment in a collection of leaky boats. At Port Talbot, they were joined by Peter Robinson and his riflemen.

James FitzGibbon longed to be with them. He would have enjoyed the 300-kilometre trip along the Lake Erie shore, with excitement guaranteed at the end. Instead, the young men of York County, untried militia, were the ones who swept this unique flotilla along at the rapid pace Brock set from his bateaux headquarters.

Drawing in Water colour & Chalk, dated 1811. Artist unknown. In possession of relatives, Guernsey.

Left: This portrait of Brock was made in Canada between 1807 and 1810, by artist Gerritt Schipper.
Right: This portrait of Tecumseh is based on a drawing by fur trader Pierre Le Dru.

Stormy weather beat upon the men and drenched them as they battled rough water under the red clay cliffs on the north shore. In the night there was no rest for men weary at the oars; the light they followed at the bow of Brock's bateau kept bobbing rapidly over the water, pressing westward.

As Brock moved through the Lake Erie night, his mind played on some American documents he had had the good luck to read. General William Hull and his weary, nervous American army of 2,500 men had marched through swampy country to the shores of Lake Erie, where Hull had hired the schooner *Cayahoga* to take their heavy baggage, medical stores, and musical instruments to Fort Detroit. But the *Cayahoga* had been captured by the British brig, *General Hunter*, and Hull's official correspondence to the secretary of war found on board. It was swiftly carried to Brock at Fort George, and it had shown in Hull a despondency and want of initiative, which cheered Brock's heart.

When Brock arrived at Amherstburg, just before midnight on August 13, he found more pleasant reading, this time brought in by Tecumseh, the Shawanese chief. With 25 warriors, Tecumseh had ambushed a party of 200 Americans sent out from Detroit to escort supplies; he had captured the provisions bound for Hull as well as another batch of Hull's letters, still full of doubt and fear.

The meeting of Brock and Tecumseh, as it comes to us through the pen and paintbrush of those who watched, is one of the dramatic moments in Canadian history. Each had heard of the other. The general stood six-foot-three and broad-shouldered in his scarlet tunic and white pants, his eyes blue and steady in a strong but amiable face framed by fair hair; the Shawanese chief was smaller but supple and perfectly built. His copper face was oval, his hair shining black over dark, piercing eyes that took the measure of Brock. Born within a year of one another, but with backgrounds worlds apart, fate was joining their destinies and they both seemed to know it. (They would die within a year of each other, too.) From the moment of their meeting a unique rapport was evident between them. Tecumseh smiled and said to one of his party in his mother tongue, "This is a man!" On a later occasion, Tecumseh's perceptive admiration of Brock's character was expressed in terse, simple words, "Other chiefs say, 'Go' — General Brock says, 'Come.'"[7]

The day after their first meeting, Brock put his feelings for Tecumseh in a letter to Lord Liverpool, British secretary of state for war.

> He who most attracted my attention was a Shawnee Chief, Tecumseh, the brother of The Prophet, who for the last two years had carried on, contrary to our remonstrances, an active war against the United States. A more sagacious or a more gallant war-

rior does not, I believe, exist. He was the admiration of everyone who conversed with him.[8]

It was Tecumseh who supplied Brock with details of the terrain around Fort Detroit. (Hull had withdrawn from Sandwich across the river into his fort on August 7.) On a roll of bark, Tecumseh's scalping knife drew the river, then the hills, the clearings, the muskeg and forest, and network of trails that would serve Brock's little army. But that night, in private council, Brock was unable to convince Colonel Henry Procter and his other officers to attack. Procter had 250

Tecumseh's People

Tecumseh's father was a Shawnee but the Natives he led were of many tribes: Kickapoo, Potawatomie, Wyandot, Creek, Delaware, Sauk, and Winnebago. With his brother, Tenskwatawa, known as "The Prophet," Tecumseh sought to organize the tribes into a confederacy to resist White encroachment on their lands.

The brothers travelled from tribe to tribe urging a return to traditional ways and a rejection of White culture, especially liquor, which they saw destroying village life.

In 1811, Tecumseh's own village on the Tippecanoe River had about 700 warriors. William Henry Harrison, the Indiana territorial governor, led his troops onto Native land to attack while Tecumseh was away preaching to Creek tribes in the south.

After coming home to find his village wiped out, a bitter and angry Tecumseh led his people north into Canada. After his warriors took part in the victories at Detroit and Fort Meigs, more tribes joined him, until he had 3,000 Natives ready to fight for the British cause.

But when Procter gave up Fort Meigs and moved back into Canada, many of these newcomers slipped away home. As Procter retreated farther inland, Tecumseh talked him into a stand on the Thames River — it was there that Tecumseh was killed.

Only 700 of Tecumseh's men followed the retreating British Army to Burlington Heights and Niagara. These disheartened tribesmen did little fighting and were an added burden on army rations.

regulars at Amherstburg and 150 militia. Altogether they would have 300 regulars and 400 militia. Suddenly, Brock stopped the useless arguing and announced that he had made a decision. They would cross the river and attack Fort Detroit.

When the Natives were told of his decision, Tecumseh remarked that their great father, King George, had awakened out of a long sleep. Tecumseh's hatred of the Americans knew no bounds and the men of the 5th U.S. Regiment, who were holding Fort Detroit, were his special enemies. Less than a year before, under General Harrison, they had slaughtered Tecumseh's half-armed band of 600 men and women on the banks of the Tippecanoe River while he and his warriors were away.

That afternoon, Brock moved to Sandwich, opposite Fort Detroit, and occupied the mansion of Colonel Baby. Lieutenant-Colonel Macdonell and Major J.B. Glegg, his two aides-de-camp, were sent off to Hull with a dispatch demanding immediate surrender. "It is far from my intention to join in a war of extermination," Brock had written, "but you must be aware that the numerous body of Indians who have attached themselves to my troops will be beyond control the moment the contest commences."[9] In actual fact, Brock had a promise from Tecumseh that the scalping knife would not be used the next day, and Tecumseh was rare among North American chiefs in that he did not use torture.

The trails north of Sandwich, visible from Fort Detroit, were alive with marching men. They were the same men, marching back and forth, crossing and re-crossing — Brock's few soldiers and Tecumseh's braves attempting to make their army look double its actual size. Major Thomas Evans had craftily clothed the western militia in cast-off uniforms of the 41st Regiment, giving them twice the number of regulars in the eyes of the Americans.

During the previous week, soldiers had worked under dark of night to set up a battery in a grove of oak trees opposite Fort Detroit. By the time Brock received Hull's answer that he would not surrender, the battery was ready. On the night of August 15, the trees were cut down. The next morning, Brock's force of 330 regulars and 400 militia, with 600 Natives under Tecumseh, crossed the Detroit River. Slowly, the columns were formed, and the steady tramp of determined men sounded

Enid Mallory.

At Fort Detroit Brock marched his men along paths and through woods over and over again to make their numbers look big.

on the trails to Fort Detroit. Two 24-pounders that Hull had placed in their path, and the long heavy guns of Fort Detroit, looked them in the eyes and waited.

Meanwhile, the batteries, revealed to the Americans by the morning light, opened fire. The first shot fired in the War of 1812 crashed into the American fort and killed an American officer who was a close friend of the British artillerymen who trained the gun. Now Hull's 24-pounders answered the British guns and shells, and round shot flew in both directions across the river. An 18-pound shell from one of the British guns crashed through an embrasure in the officers' mess and killed four men. Hull made up his mind.

The British troops, expecting grapeshot and hellfire at any second as they advanced, saw instead a white flag. Simultaneously, another white flag was crossing the river to silence the Sandwich battery. It was over. Hull was surrendering his army of 2,500 to 330 British, 400 militia, and 600 Natives.

CHAPTER 4
QUEENSTON HEIGHTS

Every three or four miles, on every eminence, Brock has erected a snug bat-
tery, the last saucy argument of kings, poking their white noses and round
black nostrils right upon your face, ready to spit fire and brimstone in your
very teeth, if you were to offer to turn squatter on John Bull's land.
— John Lovett (General Van Rensselaer's military secretary) to Joseph
Alexander, Lewiston, 1812[1]

After the victory at Detroit, Captain Glegg carried dispatches and the colour of
the 4th U.S. Regiment to Sir George Prevost in the city of Quebec. As he passed,
people in the streets of York, Kingston, and Montreal walked a little taller. There
was rowdy laughter in the barrack rooms at Niagara and Kingston. Lieutenant
George Ryerson, bearing the news to the Talbot settlement, stopped for the night
in a Native camp where aged warriors and women chanted songs of victory all
night. And on the St. Lawrence the rhythm of the bateaux was halted as men
threw their arms in the air and cheers resounded over the water.

From Fort George, an urgent message was sent to Kingston asking for three
companies of the 49th Regiment and a detachment of the Newfoundland Regiment. The hourly expected arrival of the prisoners from Detroit might place Fort
George in the awkward position of having more prisoners than soldiers.

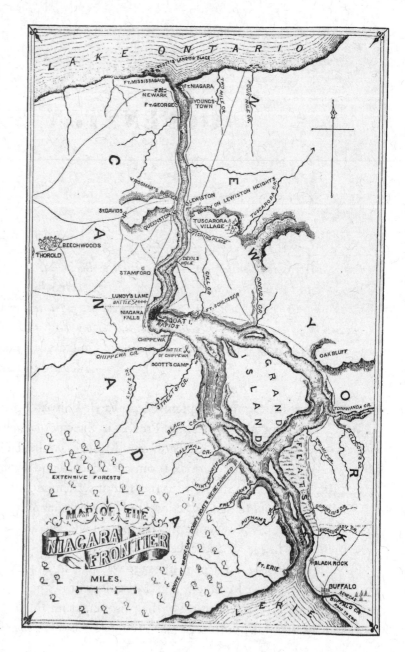

The Niagara frontier.

Fort George, situated on the west bank of the Niagara River about two kilometres from Lake Ontario and opposite the American Fort Niagara, consisted of six small bastions connected by picket fencing 3.5 metres high, with room for 220 men and a spacious officers' quarters. The town of Newark (Niagara-on-the-Lake) nestled against its rather dubious protection. Vessels of over 45 tonnes could sail past Newark up the Niagara River as far as Queenston, where the portage around Niagara Falls began. Even without war, this portage road was a bustling street with salt pork and flour and trading goods arriving, while North West Company furs from the west as well as wheat, corn, oats, and fruit from the Niagara farms, moved down.

But on August 25 a parade of victory came down the Queenston road as the Detroit expedition returned. We can see it most clearly from the American side where no one described it better than John Lovett, secretary to General Van Rensselaer. Lovett always turned the light of humour on those pompous British across the river. He shone an equally brilliant searchlight on the humiliation of his fellow Americans.

> It [yesterday] was a day of turmoil, mortification and humiliation through out our camp. Such a flood as the consequences of Gen. Hull's surrender poured in upon us that it required considerable nerve to meet everything … Yesterday the first we saw was a guard of about 50 men passing with some wagons on the opposite shore; it was the victorious Brock returning to Fort George. He sent over Col. McDonald [Macdonell], his aide-de-camp, and Major Evans, two strapping lads in scarlet, gold and arms, to make a communication to General Van Rensselaer.
>
> I was ever proud of my country, and as an American could look any man of any nation at least horizontally in the face. But yesterday my eyes seemed to have acquired a new attachment to the ground.
>
> … Before and behind, on the right and on the left, their proud victors gleamed in arms and their heads erect in the pride of vic-

tory … I think the line, including wagons, pleasure carriages, etc., was half a mile long, scattered. The sensation this scene produced in our camp were inexpressible, mortification, indignation, fearful apprehension, suspicion, jealousy, dismay, rage, madness.[2]

American leaders had planned to draw the closing curtains swiftly on this Canadian play. One Massachusetts general officer had offered to "capture Canada by contract, raise a company of soldiers and take it in six weeks." Or, as Dearborn had written to Van Rensselaer, "At all events we must calculate on possessing Canada before the winter sets in." Now these men were stunned.

Aboard the schooner *Chippewa*, while sailing down Lake Erie, Isaac Brock had suffered a rude shock himself. The schooner *Lady Prevost* had hailed his ship and brought news of an armistice. Brock, with plans already in his head for taking Fort Niagara, exploded in anger. An armistice was a stupid blunder that would give the Americans time to transport stores and men to the Niagara frontier, building their naval power on the lakes. Brock believed (and most historians agree) that he could have taken Fort Niagara. Prevost, however, still believed that peace was possible. Britain's irritating orders-in-council had been repealed and Prevost believed that meant that war could be avoided. But impressment was still an issue. Prevost also failed to understand the American belief in "manifest destiny," their conviction that all of North America should be theirs.

On September 4, Kingston greeted the arrival of Brock with spontaneous celebration. Fitz may have been there and it may have been the last time the two men met. More likely, Fitz was taking advantage of September weather on the river. Twelve days later, on September 16, he was taking a convoy upriver when he was attacked near Prescott, where the St. Lawrence is at its narrowest. Americans at Ogdensburg opposite Prescott outfitted a Durham boat and a gunboat and landed in the night on Toussaint Island, near the British boats. The family living on the island was captured, but one man escaped and swam to the Canadian shore to alarm FitzGibbon and rally the local militia.

When Friends Fight

People on opposite sides of this border war were friends, even relatives. But once the war started they were also enemies. Major John Lovett described it best:

> *If any man wants to see folly triumphant, let him come here, let him view friends by friends stretched for hundreds of miles on these two shores, all loving and beloved; all desirous of harmony; all wounded by being coerced, by a hand unseen, to cut throats ... the sponge of time can never wipe this blot from the American name....*

Lovett himself had been drawn into the war. A lawyer by profession, he was aide and secretary to his friend, Major-General Stephen Van Rensselaer. During the attack on Queenston, Lovett was put in charge of the guns above Lewiston. When the battle was over he would discover that he had been made permanently deaf.

There were Canadians with American backgrounds and American sympathies who became spies and informers. That Americans and Canadians speak the same language greatly added to the confusion. All it took was a coat borrowed from a dead enemy to pass yourself off as one of the enemy, a ruse that FitzGibbon often used to gain the upper hand and take prisoners.

Americans along the lower St. Lawrence and in all the northeastern states had not been able to work up much hatred for their Canadian neighbours. Apart from any ties of the heart, they were Yankees and not prone to pass up an opportunity to make a dollar. As the war went on and the British became short of supplies, the opportunities for making money got better and better.

John Le Couteur was 18 in 1813, when he served as a light infantry officer in the 104th Regiment. At Niagara, he was often sent with messages to the Americans in Fort George under a flag of truce. He became friends with some of the officers and even shared a meal with one. In his memoir, he wrote, "How uncomfortably like a civil war it seemed when we were in good humoured friendly converse...."[3]

When the Americans attacked, soldiers and militia were ready for them. In the fray the Yankees had to abandon their Durham boat, which drifted into Canadian hands. When the American gunboat and brigade exchanged fire, five of the 18 men on the gunboat were wounded. When the others on board turned a cannon on the British, FitzGibbon had to move his boats out of range. By that time, the Americans had had enough and scurried back to Ogdensburg with their wounded.

On September 18, from Niagara, Brock wrote of his old regiment, "Six companies of the 49th are with me here, and the remaining four at Kingston, under Vincent. Although the regiment has been 10 years in this country, drinking rum without bounds, it is still respectable and·apparently ardent for an opportunity to acquire distinction."

President Madison ended the armistice on September 18, increasing the tension along the 58-kilometre border from Fort George to Fort Erie. Brock kept his officers galloping along the river road to the guns at Brown's Point and Voorman's Point to Queenston, Chippawa, and Fort Erie, in a frenzy of organizing, dispatching, informing and reviewing, tightening and strengthening, in whatever way he could, their thin red line of defence.

On October 9, at Fort Erie, where the Niagara River flows out of Lake Erie, Lieutenant Elliot, an enterprising young American, attacked and boarded the brigs *Detroit* and *Caledonia*. The *Detroit* was an American ship taken from General Hull at Detroit; the *Caledonia* a brig of the North West Fur Company. Elliot's party managed to get the *Caledonia* over to the American batteries at Black Rock. The *Detroit* they burned when the firing from the Fort Erie garrison became too hot. Elliot gave the Americans their first shot of confidence since Hull's defeat.

On the night of October 11, a tremendous northeast storm brought thunder, lightning, and rain in torrents. Rain was still coming down as Brock and his staff sat late in council on the night of the 12th. Then, at 4:15 in the morning of the 13th, Brock was awakened by cannon fire and recognized the noise of the big gun at Voorman's Point. Within moments he was on his horse Alfred and away, orders left behind to "Inform Colonel Macdonell and Major Glegg that I am off for Queenston. They are to follow, with all speed."

Brock made the 11-kilometre ride from Fort George to Queenston on his horse, Alfred, in the dark and stormy pre-dawn hours of October 13, 1812.

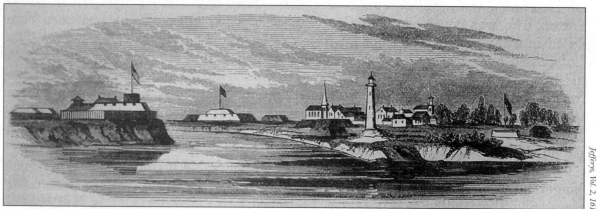

Jefferys, Vol. 2, 161.

This view shows the entrance to the Niagara River and the positions of forts George and Niagara.

The 11-kilometre ride, along the river road from Fort George to Queenston, was Brock's last. His cloak streamed behind him as his horse pounded through the pre-dawn gloom. The dawn, when it came, would be spectacular, lighting up the mist over the blue Niagara and sending horizontal light through the coloured trees, iridescent and alive with rain and wind.

Brock's ears were tuned to the guns. Their different notes created a sound picture of what was happening, the 24-pounder at Voorman's Point answering the guns of Lewiston across the river, the more distant punctuation of the 3-pounders and the brass 7-pounders at Queenston, and the roar of the 18-pounder that was halfway up Queenston Heights in a V-shaped redan battery. At Brown's Point, three kilometres below Queenston, he found the company of York Volunteers on the move toward Queenston, and waved them on. He galloped past the big gun at Voorman's. Samuel Peter Jarvis of the York Volunteers galloped past Brock on a horse bound for Fort George, and told the general, "The Americans are crossing the river in force, sir."

Lights were burning in all the houses as women and children huddled together. The bells of the church and courthouse at Niagara were ringing. In pursuit of Brock, his two aides, Macdonell and Glegg, spurred their horses along the river road.

Lossing, 390.

Queenston in 1812 was a tiny town nestled below Queenston Heights.

Brock reached the Niagara Escarpment where the land rises 91 metres above the village of Queenston. Niagara Falls tumbled over here 12,000 years ago before it wore itself back 11 kilometres to its present site, forming the Niagara Gorge as it retreated. Brock galloped through the village and halfway up Queenston Heights for a view of what was happening on the river below. It was daylight and more than a thousand Americans had landed and sought shelter under the brow of the Heights, awaiting reinforcements. The 49th Grenadiers under Dennis and the York Militia with a 3-pounder were near the river, firing on the invaders. High on the Heights, Captain Williams had the 49th Light Infantry behind the 18-pounder pouring down destruction on the boats trying to cross the river. Then Brock ordered Williams's company down the hill to help Dennis.

Down at the river, a young American, Captain Wool, saw the British movement down the hill and, in a bold stroke, took his men up a fisherman's path, supposedly unassailable, to arrive 27 metres above the redan battery. When he saw American blue above him, Brock had no choice. He spiked the gun and his 12 men at the battery fled down the hill, leaving the Americans in command of Queenston Heights.

With Williams's company behind him, Brock attempted to take back the Heights. George Jarvis was there, and tells what happened:

> On arriving at the foot of the mountain, where the road diverges to St. David's, General Brock dismounted, and waving his sword, climbed over a high stone wall, followed by his troops. Placing himself at the head of the light company of the 49th, he led the way up the mountain at double-quick time, in the very teeth of a sharpfire from the enemy's rifle-men, and ere long he was singled out by one of them, whom, coming forward, took deliberate aim, and fired. Several of the men noticed the action and fired, but too late, and our gallant General fell on his left side, within a few feet of where I stood. Running up to him, I enquired, "Are you much hurt sir?" He placed his hand on his breast, but made no reply, and sank down.[4]

Two flank companies of militia (the York Volunteers) were under Lieutenant-Colonel John Macdonell, Brock's aide-de-camp, at Brown's Point. Macdonell, only 25 years old, was attorney general of Upper Canada. When the news reached him, he rushed his 190 men to the Heights and tried to avenge Brock. The Americans had reinforcements by then, 500 men on the Heights. The terrible rage of Macdonell and his men forced Captain Wool back up the hill and made him spike the 18-pounder gun. But both Macdonell and Williams were seriously wounded. Macdonell's wounds were fatal, although he lived for 24 hours in great agony.

With their leaders gone, the men were in disorder. It was 10:00 a.m. and the day was already disastrous. The shattered soldiers fell back to Voorman's Point to wait for reinforcements, while the Americans conveyed wounded across the river and brought over fresh troops. The death of Brock had stunned every man. His body lay nearby in Durham's farmhouse. Macdonell lay there too, dying. The dreadful news swept along the frontier.

Captain Driscoll of the 100th Regiment wrote about how a dragoon galloped up to Fort Erie and gave the news to an "old Green Tiger" who seemed unable to tell it to his comrades:

> I placed my hand on his shoulder, "For heaven's sake, tell us what you know." In choking accents he revealed his melancholy information. "General Brock is killed, the enemy has possession of Queenston Heights." Every man in the battery was paralyzed. They ceased firing. A cheer from the enemy on the opposite side of the river recalled us to our duty. They had heard of their success down the river.[5]

In the other direction, the news reached Fort George, where British guns were attempting to silence the guns of Fort Niagara across the river. In command at Fort George was Major-General Roger Hale Sheaffe, whose orders from Brock were to follow as soon as he could ascertain where the enemy meant to make their real attack.

Sheaffe reached Voorman's at about eleven o'clock, then took a back route through St. David's to come upon the Heights, three kilometres west of the Americans, who had a collected force of 800 men. Lieutenant John Norton (a Scotsman married to a Native girl), with 100 Natives, led Sheaffe on a route that took the Americans completely by surprise. Forced to face Sheaffe's long advancing line, the Americans found their backs to the river wall, their lives balanced on a precipice above the Niagara gorge. Sheaffe was in front of them, Queenston forces on the right, and Natives terrifying their left. Wool was wounded and succeeded by Colonel Winfield Scott, who tried to keep his men in order.

Across the river at Lewiston, General Van Rensselaer was attempting to get reinforcements to his men on Queenston Heights. His secretary, Lovett, gives us an idea of how it was over there:

> Still the reinforcements moved over very slowly and, in short, stopped. The General returned to accelerate them. He mounted a borrowed horse and I rode with him, everywhere urging on the troops, for not half of them had passed over. But the name of Indian, or the sight of the wounded, or the devil or something else petrified them. Not a regiment, not a company, scarcely a man would go.[6]

The Americans on the Heights were in complete panic. They fled down the cliff and attempted to swim the Niagara. Many threw themselves off the Heights. At three o'clock, Colonel Winfield Scott raised the white flag and surrendered 300 soldiers and officers to the British. Six hundred more would be rooted out of hiding the following day.

The bright joy of victory was darkened by overwhelming grief at the death of Brock. For less than two months the Canadas had had a larger-than-life hero. Now they had a dead hero.

In the dark hours of the night, Brock's surviving aide-de-camp sat alone writing a letter to Mr. William Brock:

> With a heart agonized with most painful sorrow, I am compelled by duty and affection to announce to you the death of my most valuable and ever to be lamented friend, your brother, Major-General Brock ... His loss at any time would have been great to his relations and friends, but at this moment I consider the melancholy event as a public calamity. He was beloved and esteemed by all who had the happiness to know him, and was adored by his army and by the inhabitants of the Province.[7]

In Story and Song

The War of 1812 inspired patriotic verse that was sometimes set to music and sung by those who remembered the war. Two verses from The Battle of Queenston Heights are typical:

His loyal-hearted soldiers were ready every one,
Their foes were thrice their number, but duty must be done.
They started up the fire-swept hill with loud resounding cheers,
While Brock's inspiring voice rang out, "Push on, York Volunteers!"

Each true Canadian soldier laments the death of Brock;
His country told its sorrow in monumental rock;
And if a foe should e're invade our land in future years,
His dying words will guide us still, "Push on, brave Volunteers!"[7]

General Brock and Lieutenant-Colonel Macdonell were buried on October 17 in the northeast battery at Fort George. The coffins were preceded first by a company of regulars and a band of music, and followed by another body of regulars and militia. The distance between Government House and the garrison was lined by a double row of militia men and Natives, resting on their arms reversed. Minute guns were fired during the whole procession. Across the river, the Americans fired minute-guns at Lewiston and Fort Niagara "as a mark of respect to a brave enemy."

Van Rensselaer had been opposed to this war in the first place; within days he resigned and handed over the Niagara command to General Smythe.

Major-General Sheaffe, Brock's successor, had agreed to another armistice without any apparent reason. It was not approved by Sir George Prevost, who seemed to finally understand Brock's position once Brock was dead. The armistice applied only to the Niagara frontier between Lakes Erie and Ontario and could be terminated on 24 hours notice. It lasted until the Americans ended it on November 20.

For the month after Brock's death, Upper Canada could talk of nothing else. There were a few who ventured the suggestion that Brock was rash, that he should have protected his own life and lived to fight another day — and many historians today agree. But the question remains: without the gallant example of that scarlet figure out in front, would the Canadas have struggled to their feet at all? Without a hero who could size up the desperate odds and attempt desperate measures, had they any chance against the American giant?

If anyone understood Brock's fighting philosophy, it was the men of the 49th Regiment. Trained in the tactics of speed and surprise, they admired honesty, fairness, and personal bravery. The "old Green Tiger" at Fort Erie, who was stunned to silence by the news of Brock's death, had quickly recovered himself and he and his comrades "exhibited demoniac energy" as their guns gave it to Black Rock "hot and heavy."

This demoniac energy was to characterize the 49th Regiment in the two hard years of fighting ahead. Brock was somehow their leader in death as he had been in life. His scarlet figure beckoning up the heights of Queenston seemed to stand before them, whether at Niagara or Stoney Creek or Crysler's Farm on the St. Lawrence.

And from Detroit the words of Tecumseh rang out, "Other chiefs say, 'Go' — General Brock says, 'Come.'"

CHAPTER 5

ON THE NIAGARA FRONTIER

FitzGibbon was a fine man and a splendid soldier. The men adored him, although he was strict. His word was law, and they had such faith in him that I believe if he had told any one of them to jump into the river, he would have obeyed. He always knew what he was about, and his men knew it, and had full confidence in him.

> — M. Le Lievre, of Trois Rivières, speaking in 1873 of convoy expeditions in 1812[1]

However great the shock and grief of its losses, an army must march on. Battles might wait for spring, but the lifeline of supply still throbbed with activity in the cold of the Canadian winter. The distance from Montreal to Niagara is 720 kilometres by land (slightly less by water) with another 240 kilometres west to Amherstburg. This is a long lifeline, and if the Americans cut it at any point everything to the west of that severance would be lost. In January, a long line of sleighs could be seen making its way 400 kilometres from Kingston to Niagara, with Fitz in charge.

For a while he could keep his 45 sleighs within the shelter of what is today Prince Edward County, travelling the snow and ice of the Bay of Quinte. But once he crossed the narrow bridge of land known as the Carrying Place, his drivers

Guillet, *Pioneer Travel*, 131 (Anna Jameson).

In winter, provisions for the army had to move by sleigh on the ice or sometimes on the lakeshore road.

left all protection behind and faced the buffeting force of the January winds that swept Lake Ontario. Still, it was better there than travelling the snow-filled roads through the forests on shore. Doggedly, they kept on, thankful for days that were sparkling bright, huddling into their buffalo robes on days of whiteout blizzard.

The enthusiasm of FitzGibbon was contagious, and his men felt the challenge even as they faced the cold. The grim-visaged beauty of this land was not lost on

FitzGibbon. After 10 years in Canada he knew winter in its every mood, and its hard white beauty excited him. His affinity for the landscape and his quick commitment to memory of shorelines, contours, rivers, pathways, and roads were an important asset in the role he played in this war. Even in the white cauldron of wind on an open lake, Fitz always knew where he was.

When they reached Niagara, James stood on Queenston Heights, remembering the leader who had been like an older brother to him, a teacher, a hero, and a friend. It was some consolation to be on the Niagara frontier where Brock had died, and in a likely place for the next attack. Perhaps he could do something to reach the goal Isaac Brock had died for.

Fitz and his company were sent to the west shore of Lake Erie to guard Detroit against an American attack across the frozen lake. There had been trouble there on January 22, when the American Army of the west, under Generals Harrison and Winchester, attacked 40 kilometres south of Detroit on the River Raisin, in an attempt to take back Michigan. With his Native allies under Tecumseh, Colonel Procter had defeated them and taken 600 prisoners. Fitz probably met Tecumseh there, and it may have been from Tecumseh's warriors that Fitz learned to admire and imitate Native skills in forest warfare.

In April, FitzGibbon and his men went back to Frenchman's Creek on the Niagara River, six kilometres from Fort Erie. Winter there had been quiet, but there was news of a successful attack from Prescott on Ogdensburg, across the river, intended to stop the raiding parties that had continued since the attack on FitzGibbon's convoy the previous fall. The Canadian attackers were led by Lieutenant-Colonel "Red" George Macdonnell, a relative of John Macdonell, Brock's aide-de-camp who was slain at Queenston. His Glengarry Light Infantry Fencibles fought with the tenacity that would distinguish them throughout the war.

The spring breakup had an ominous sound that year as the big question loomed: where would the Americans attack? They had their forces positioned in three places: Plattsburgh on Lake Champlain for an attack on Montreal; Sackets Harbor, Oswego, and Niagara for attacks on Kingston, York, and Fort George; and Fort Meigs on the Maumee River, where William Henry Harrison's army was threatening the northwest.

FitzGibbon was too restless to wait for the larger action of the war. On April 6, he was scouting the river when the rays of the setting sun revealed movement on the American shore, and he saw a dugout boat move toward Strawberry Island. He and a sergeant jumped in a boat, paddled over, and "pounced on them as nose to nose, one was giving his friend a light from a cigar." Then his sharp eyes saw a second dugout leave the American shore. He hid himself close to the landing to take them prisoners as well.

But larger action was afloat on Lake Ontario. Both sides knew that whoever controlled the supply routes could win the war. On the American side, General Dearborn had command from Lake Erie to Vermont. Based at Sackets Harbor at the east end of Lake Ontario was Commodore Isaac Chauncey, who was building a sizable fleet to control Lake Ontario.

The British were apparently in for trouble. Their ships were the *Royal George*, the *Earl of Moira*, the *Sir Sidney Smith*, the *Duke of Gloucester*, and the *Prince Regent*, as well as the *Wolfe* just coming off the stocks at Kingston. Another ship, the *Sir Isaac Brock*, was being built at York. But in the race for power the Americans were pulling ahead. Moreover, the British lacked officers. Sir James Yeo, who would dance a nautical ballet with Chauncey through 1813 and 1814, was on his way to the Canadas but he would not arrive in Kingston until May 15.

The American plan was to capture Kingston and most historians believe they had it right; from there they could cut the lifeline of military supply and destroy the ships in the harbour to take control of Lake Ontario. But the Americans changed their minds. Major-General Dearborn and Commodore Isaac Chauncey fooled themselves into thinking Kingston was too well guarded and opted instead to strike York. Chauncey saw a prize there that he couldn't resist, the ship *Isaac Brock*, being built in the harbour. Capturing her would give Chauncey superior power over the British fleet.

On April 27, at seven in the morning, the American fleet under Chauncey attacked York. General Sheaffe himself was there, but his soldiers were at Fort George and along the Niagara frontier. At York he had 300 regular troops, 200 militia, and 100 Natives, as General Zebulon Pike began to land 1,700 troops

Guillet, Pioneer Settlements, 96 (Lieutenant Sempronius Stretton).

The York Barracks looked like this in 1804. They would be rebuilt after the Americans attacked Toronto, April 27, 1813.

west of old Fort Rouillé. Another thousand seamen remained on board the 14 vessels that had 100 guns trained on Fort York. Sheaffe's 700 regulars marched out of Fort York to meet the Americans on the lakeshore but soon fell back to their first battery, then their second. It was no use. They spiked the guns of the second battery and retreated into the fort.

At the second battery, Pike paused while he sent a party ahead to discover if the British had cleared out. They were gone, making a rapid march toward Kingston. Only the militia remained. Suddenly, a dreadful explosion turned the world upside down as a powder magazine exploded. The true cause of the blast has never been discovered but 100 Canadians and 250 Americans were killed or wounded. General Pike was one of them.

On the death of General Pike, General Dearborn landed. By 4:00 p.m. the American flag flew over York. Angered at the carnage of the explosion, American soldiers burned and pillaged the helpless town, including about 60 houses. Before his retreat, Sheaffe had ordered the new ship on the stocks to be burned. One other ship, the *Duke of Gloucester*, remained to be captured by the invaders.

Sheaffe would be severely criticized for his retreat, although he had little choice; his men were outnumbered three to one, the fort lacked any large guns. But he probably could have been better prepared. There were guns at York for the new ship being built, which, if mounted on the fort, might have held off Chauncey's ships.

Although he won the Battle of Queenston Heights and received a baronetcy from the British Parliament, Sheaffe would never become a hero in the Canadas. Too many soldiers, FitzGibbon among them, remembered Sheaffe's harsh treatment of his men. Others resented the armistice he signed after Queenston Heights, when he might have swept across the river to take Fort Niagara. On May 26, Sir George Prevost wrote to Lord Bathurst that he wanted to remove Sheaffe from Upper Canada. "It is my intention to place the civil administration and military command of Upper Canada in the hands of Major-General De Rottenburg, and Major-General Sir R. Sheaffe will return to Lower Canada."[2]

After the attack on York, everyone knew that Dearborn and Chauncey would waste little time before striking Fort George. In command of Lake Ontario, those two were riding a wave of confidence.

Chauncey sailed over to Fort Niagara to deposit Dearborn and his land force there on May 8, then sailed away to Sackets Harbor with his wounded and plunder from York. By May 25, Chauncey was back at Niagara, his guns firing on Fort George. Although General John Vincent had five 24-pounders from Fort Detroit, he was so short of powder that he could not answer Chauncey's guns. Reports came in to Fort George that Dearborn had 6,000 land troops in Fort Niagara, poised for the moment of attack.

Vincent had 1,400 regular soldiers and little faith in the militiamen of the province. "With respect to the militia, it is with regret that I can neither report favorably of their numbers nor their willing co-operation." He described them as "wavering and appalled by the specious force of the enemy's resources."[3]

Vincent was slow to understand the men. They were farmers and it was May, spring-planting time. Before the year was done, the British Army would be glad of every grain of wheat the men had tenaciously put in the ground that anxious spring. If Vincent thought they would stand by and give up their crops and their homes to Americans invaders, he was wrong. Soldier and settler alike were facing terrible odds, and they had no daring Isaac Brock to cheer them on. Their leader lay dead in the northeast bastion of Fort George and that knowledge sat heavy on their hearts. Nor would they find another like him throughout the war. Leaders would come and go on the Niagara frontier in 1813 and 1814, but often the impetus to win would come from below, from junior officers like James FitzGibbon, militiamen like William Hamilton Merritt, and women like Laura Secord.

Vincent's 1,400 men were divided into three divisions. Fitz was under Lieutenant-Colonel Harvey, who had command of the right, from Fort George to Brown's Point. Vincent himself was at the centre in command of the fort. On the

Sir George Prevost

Sir George Prevost served in the British Army from a young age. In 1808, he was lieutenant-governor of Nova Scotia and in 1811 was promoted to commander-in-chief of British North America. He was a cautious leader negotiating an armistice after Brock's Detroit victory, which amazed and delighted the Americans.

He visited Upper Canada in May 1813 and led a failed attack on Sackets Harbor. In 1814, he planned an attack on Lake Champlain but the British naval force was driven back and the land force had to retreat.

Although considered a failure as a field commander he was praised for his work as commander-in-chief, for his organization and preparation for defence of the Canadas.

left, along Lake Ontario to Four Mile Creek, was Colonel Myers. Early on the morning of May 27, a thick fog on the lake shrouded the American ships as they landed 6,000 troops under Colonel Winfield Scott.

Within three hours the contest was decided. The British left wing, under Colonel Myers, had suffered severely from the troops landing and the fire from the ships. Fort George and the entire peninsula-plateau were caught in crossfire from the lake and the mouth of the river; the log buildings of the fort were on fire. At twelve o'clock, Major Glegg wrote a hasty note to Colonel William Claus at Fort George: "The General desires you will immediately evacuate the Fort and join him in the Queenston road." The guns of Fort George were spiked, the ammunition destroyed, and the troops put in motion to march 29 kilometres across country to the house of John DeCew near the Beaver Dams.

The weary soldiers retreated in good order, the rearguard holding off the Americans now taking possession of the Niagara frontier. In the houses of Newark and Queenston, women and children clung together facing the terrible decision to abandon their homes or stay within enemy lines. The rearguard reached De-Cew's sometime during the night and were soon joined by Lieutenant-Colonel Bisshopp with all the troops from Chippawa to Fort Erie.

In the morning, Vincent found "all the militia of the country" flocking to him at DeCew's. If the British Army was ready to retreat, the militia was not. William Hamilton Merritt, settled at the mouth of the Twelve Mile Creek near where St. Catharines is today, was 19 when war broke out and, as a militia dragoon, he committed himself to the cause. He and the rest of the militia expected that:

> … we would give them battle and prevent their penetrating in
> the country. However, to our great surprise and annoyance, an
> order was issued for all the wagons to be impressed and the army
> to retreat to the Forty [Mile Creek]. As many of the militia as
> chose to follow might, the rest were at liberty to return to their
> respective families. I strongly suspected from the indifferent
> manner the militia were treated the upper part of the Province

was to be abandoned, as did all the militia, consequently numbers went home.... [4]

At least one British soldier agreed with the militiamen who wanted to fight. FitzGibbon could not believe they were giving up the Niagara Peninsula. But Vincent, pushed by an advancing American Army, was moving all the way back to Burlington.

He had a strong position there, on the height of land at the end of Burlington Bay where Dundurn Castle stands today in the city of Hamilton. Facing the bay, and with the Desjardins Marsh behind, this isthmus of land, 30 metres above the water, was unassailable except across a narrow neck of land bristling with field guns. Legend has it that the Duke of Wellington, studying a map of Upper Canada, put his finger on Burlington Heights as the place he would

The Reverend John Strachan

John Strachan arrived in Upper Canada in 1799, and became a tutor in Kingston while he studied for a position in the Episcopalian church. He was ordained in 1803 and became rector of Cornwall, where he established the grammar school that would educate the sons of well-to-do loyalists. In 1811, he moved to York to be rector and chaplain of the garrison and, again, started a school.

When the American fleet attacked York and General Sheaffe moved his troops toward Kingston, leaving the militia in charge, Strachan took over, marching forth to meet the invaders. He hassled Commodore Chauncey and accused General Dearborn of stalling negotiations so his men could pillage and burn to town. He actually made the Americans return some of the stolen goods.

Strachan went on to become the first bishop of Toronto. He also served on the executive council and continued to educate the leaders of Upper Canada. He was a great organizer, absolutely convinced of his God-given mandate — to keep Canada British and hold off the forces of democracy, liberalism, and reform. If the Family Compact had a central core, Strachan was it.

choose to defend. Here, Vincent would try to hold the British Army together against the advancing enemy.

But he did not want the militia there. It had been "like drawing their eye teeth" to call them out a month before, now he did not know how to get rid of them. Lieutenant Harvey, writing at Burlington to Major Titus G. Simons, commanding the Incorporated Militia, expressed admiration for the gallant conduct of the militia in the neighbourhood of Fort George but explained how Vincent felt they could best promote the cause:

> It is not by joining us as a military body that your cause can at this moment be best advanced. When our reinforcements have all arrived and all other arrangements matured for repossessing ourselves of the country we have for the moment yielded, and for driving the invader far back into his own settlements, then will the gallant militia of Upper Canada be called upon to join and add inestimable strength in our ranks.[5]

But things would not happen quite that way. The soldiers were as eager to fight as the militia, and Lieutenant-Colonel John Harvey, working with men like James FitzGibbon, would do something about it. History could call their daring attack the Battle of Stoney Creek.

CHAPTER 6
THE BATTLE OF STONEY CREEK

I wish some of your merchants would be enterprising enough to send us up supplies of shoes, shirts, stockings, &c, &c. Not one in 20 has an article more than what is on his person. Adieu.
— Lieutenant James FitzGibbon to the Reverend James Somerville of Montreal. Burlington Bay, June 7, 1813[1]

General Vincent's army had worn out its shoes. On May 31, he wrote from Bazeley's farmhouse, Head of the Lake, "We want everything — shoes, stockings, blankets, tents and shirts. I have wrote to York to forward me all they may have at that post."[2]

Even worse, they lacked ammunition. There were 90 rounds remaining to each man, and with York fallen to the enemy and Chauncey's fleet hovering like a bird of prey on Lake Ontario, there was little hope of getting more.

Vincent had his whole force of 1,600 men falling back to the Head of the Lake. By June 5, the American Army of about 2,500, including 250 cavalry and eight guns, under Generals Chandler and Winder, had reached Forty Mile Creek (now Grimsby). The British rearguard had been camping at Stoney Creek, near Lake Ontario, about 11 kilometres from Burlington Heights, and had to fall back with the main body on the Heights. Scouts brought the news to Vincent that the Americans were preparing to camp at Stoney Creek.

Sir John Harvey

John Harvey was the son of a clergyman who, like FitzGibbon, had to achieve promotion in the army through patronage, diligence, and talent rather than wealth, aristocratic connection, or military background. In June 1812, he was promoted to lieutenant-colonel and arrived in Canada to serve as adjutant general to General Vincent. No laggard, he crossed New Brunswick on snowshoes in the middle of winter to get to his work in Upper Canada.

The night attack at Stoney Creek, led by Harvey, secured his reputation in the army. His flexible, tolerant manner made him a favourite with those who served under him; FitzGibbon always spoke of him as a competent leader. His duties included organizing and working with both the militia and the Native tribes, as well as reconnaissance.

In his later career, he served as lieutenant-governor of New Brunswick, of Nova Scotia, and of Newfoundland. In 1824, he was honoured with a knighthood.

History does not agree on who suggested a night attack to Colonel Harvey, or who spied out the American camp. Merritt said the suggestion was made by Cornet McKenney, one of his Dragoons, or by Mr. George, an ensign in the militia. FitzGibbon's granddaughter, Agnes FitzGibbon, says that it was James FitzGibbon who did the spying. The incident is so in keeping with his madcap courage and the comic streak in this character that it is tempting to believe her.

She says that he volunteered to learn the exact position and disposition of the camp and that he did it by disguising himself as a settler and selling butter to the Americans. "There is no doubt whatever that he made himself very entertaining to the soldiers, to whom he sold all his butter, getting the best price for it."

Agnes FitzGibbon says he let the Americans think he was giving them valuable information (all of it erroneous) on the state of affairs in the British camp. In fact, he was seeing and hearing all that the British needed to know about the American camp. Meanwhile, a young lad named Billy Green had learned the American password. Both FitzGibbon and Billy Green hurried to Burlington

The Adventures of Billy Green

If anyone actually enjoyed the War of 1812, it was Billy Green. Born on the Niagara Escarpment, he roamed the ravines and paths and knew every cave and lookout. He was 19 when he heard that the Americans were coming and, with his brother Levi, set out to see for himself. When they saw the troops moving below the escarpment, Billy and Levi terrified them with war whoops, then ran off. They came upon a lone soldier, hit him with a stick, and got themselves fired upon. They made their way to Levi's house on the edge of the mountain and watched the soldiers arrive at Stoney Creek, getting shot at again.

Billy went to check on his sister Keziah, and discovered that her husband, Isaac Corman, had been taken prisoner. Billy went to look for Isaac, heard his owl-hoot signal, and met him in the woods. Isaac described what happened after his capture:

> *The major and I got to talking and he said he was second cousin to General Harrison. I said I was a first cousin of General Harrison [which was true] and came from Kentucky. After a little longer a message came for the major; he said "I must go: you may go home Corman." I said I couldn't get through the lines. He said "I will give you the countersign," and he did.*

Isaac gave the countersign to Billy, who took Levi's horse, Tip, and rode off to Burlington Heights, where he told his story to Colonel Harvey.

Once Harvey had the password, as well as a layout of the camp that Fitz had drawn, he started his men marching toward Stoney Creek. Billy Green, who assured them he knew every inch of the area, was given a sword and led the way. He said the men kept falling behind. "I told them it would be daylight before we got there if we did not hurry. Someone said it would be soon enough to be killed."

After the battle, Billy and his neighbours got oxen and a stone boat and helped to bury the dead soldiers on a knoll near the road at Stoney Creek.[3]

Heights with their information. Fitz was convinced that a night attack would work. Harvey took the plan to Vincent and, after deliberation, Vincent agreed upon it.

There was little time to lose. In the morning, the Americans would attack them and with their superior numbers they would force the British to flee and abandon the peninsula. Colonel Procter and the whole western country would then fall to the Americans. They had only that night to change the course of history.

At eleven o'clock, the men who were already asleep on the grass were awakened and the march toward the enemy started. A brief rain shower fell on the men as they started through the pitch-dark night.

FitzGibbon was commanding the 5th company from the head of the column. He says they had about 700 men, Merritt says 590. When they were five kilometres out, the march was stopped and the men were told they were undertaking a night attack. At this point the loading was drawn from each man's gun.

Fitz knew as he withdrew the flint from his own gun that this would cost lives. Men would have to stand under enemy fire and concentrate on the awkward task of replacing a flint. Many would fall without succeeding. But it had to be. James knew very well the excitable Irish temperament of the Green Tigers. It would take only one man with a flint in his gun to fire too soon to bring disaster upon them all.

Fitz talked to his company, explaining what lay ahead and urging them to depend on the vicious silence of the bayonet. He could feel the tense awareness of his men, the controlled fear, the readiness to face death in the dark of night, rather than wait for poorer odds tomorrow. The march went on, eastward along Burlington Bay. It was nearly two o'clock in the warm, damp, silent night when the ghost-like column of moving men reached Stoney Creek. The enforced quiet had drawn nerves taut.

In a diagram drawn later by FitzGibbon, the Americans are shown camped in Gage's fields at the base of a six-metre hill, 500 of them to the left of the road leading to Gage's house, 2,000 on the right. Their guns were on the brow of the hill, positioned in the road. Pickets were half a mile ahead, in the woods.

Enid Mallory.

The Americans manned their guns from a six-metre hill at the base of the escarpment.

The first two sentries were silently made prisoners. The third resisted and was bayoneted. His cries alerted the men of the next picket at the entrance to the cleared field and one of them fired a shot. By then the first two companies of the column were upon the 500 men to the left of the road. Surprise was complete until, suddenly, the officers in the front began cheering. The soldiers took up the cry, the tension of their silent march broken, bid absolute bedlam resulted. FitzGibbon was furious:

I was aware that it would be almost impossible to make the men silent again, and that consequently orders could not be heard or obeyed. I instantly turned to my men and charged them not to take up the shout then coming from the front, and by the assistance of my three sergeants, I succeeded in keeping them silent and in good order until a late stage of the affair, when firing on our side became general. Then, shouting, we rushed into the open ground occupied by the enemy and wheeled to the left.

The Americans ran from their campfires to the hill behind. The 2,000 on the right of the road opened a tremendous fire upon the British soldiers who were "endeavouring to form in extreme darkness upon unknown and rough ground covered with rail fences, fallen trees and stumps." Still worse, the British were caught in the light from the campfires while the Americans had gained the darkness on the hill.

Our men never ceased shouting. No order could be heard. Everything was noise and confusion — which confusion was chiefly occasioned by the noise. Our men returned fire contrary to orders and it soon became apparent that it was impossible to prevent shouting and firing. The scene at this instant was awfully grand. The darkness of the morning, 2 o'clock, made still more dark by the flashing of the musketry and cannon. The officers could no longer control their men and they soon began to fall back.

Suddenly, Major Plenderleath of the 49th decided on charging the guns that were firing down the road upon them. With part of FitzGibbon's company and a few other men, he rushed the guns and took all four of them. The two American generals, Chandler and Winder, were made prisoners, along with five field officers and captains, and 100 other prisoners. With the British at the top of the hill right in their centre, the Americans broke and fled — just in time, for the British were fleeing too.

Jeffrys, Vol. 2, 161.

C.W. JEFFERYS

The Battle of Stoney Creek, as depicted by C.W. Jeffreys, shows the 49th Regiment charging the guns.

The total confusion and the terror of night fighting had almost finished them. Fitz said, "I am of the opinion that had not Major Plenderleath made the dash he did the Americans would have kept their ground and our ruin would have been inevitable."

Daylight comes early to Stoney Creek in June, and the daylight would have revealed to the Americans how few British soldiers actually made up the screaming, cheering hell that had come upon them in the night. Colonel Harvey prudently withdrew his men from the field in the last shreds of darkness.

General Vincent was lost. Harvey sent William Hamilton Merritt to search for him among the dead and wounded strewn for three kilometres along the road and into the woods. Challenged by an American sentry near Gage's house, Merritt almost became a prisoner. But his blue jacket and password let him pretend he was one of the Americans. By this ruse he took the American prisoner, then captured a second who came up. But he found no Vincent, either dead or alive. FitzGibbon, who rarely spoke well of Vincent, said,

> General Vincent with the whole left of the line retreated, or I may say fled into the woods, and not until noon next day did we know what was become of him. A flag of truce was sent to inquire if he was taken but the Americans knew nothing of him. Natives were sent in search of him but without success. He at length found a road and joined us. Numbers of officers and men were lost for a time in the woods, so difficult is it to navigate these forests.[4]

Two thousand more Americans had been landed by Chauncey's ships on the lakeshore the evening before, and during the day they made their way to the now-deserted battlefield. They burnt whatever had not yet been carried off by the British, then they joined their main body falling back to Forty Mile Creek.

By the 7th, the Natives had heard what happened and according to Merritt "they came on in droves." The militia, who had been sent home by Vincent, swarmed out again to make prisoners of any Americans still lost in the woods. At six o'clock that night the Americans at Forty Mile Creek thought they saw

Enid Mallory.

This British firing line is re-enacting the Battle of Stoney Creek.

Chauncey's sails appear on the silver sheet of Lake Ontario. There was great rejoicing until they could make out the flags — then dismay. The ships were British! Sir James Yeo had set sail from Kingston on June 3, and was making his first public appearance before a large and unappreciative audience.

Prevost had already led Yeo to attack Sackets Harbor while the American fleet was attacking Fort George, but nothing decisive had been accomplished there. Although he could not bring his ships close to the shore at Forty Mile Creek, he was sending his gunboats in with a sharp and well-directed fire against the batteries the Americans had set up. Meanwhile, the Natives had taken up a position on the escarpment behind the Americans to discomfit them even more.

Enid Mallory.

Billy Green's brick house on the escarpment was built six years after the end of the war.

On the 8th, Yeo sent in a note demanding the surrender of the American Army, and the Americans decided on a full retreat by land to Fort George. They tried to send some baggage and camp equipment by bateaux, but 17 of them were captured by a British schooner.

When Lieutenant-Colonel Bisshopp's advance party arrived, they found 500 tents still standing, 140 barrels of flour, 100 stand of arms, a considerable amount of other stores, and 70 prisoners. He did not say whether they found any shoes for the ragged British Army.

Afterward, people on the Niagara Peninsula would tell how it took the Americans four days to make their way up to Stoney Creek, less than one day to run back.

CHAPTER 7
GREEN TIGER GUERRILLAS

A wonderful change has taken place in our prospects since the nocturnal visit
to the enemy's encampment at Stoney Creek on the 6th. We begin to carry on
our arrangements as usual. We are all well and in the highest spirits.
— Major J.B. Glegg to William Jarvis, Forty Mile Creek, June 15, 1813[1]

In spite of the general rejoicing ("a Royal Salute was fired in Kingston in celebration of the splendid achievement"), FitzGibbon was not satisfied. According to his granddaughter, he thought the British should have pursued the retreating Americans and recovered Fort George. Nor did the exploit at Stoney Creek meet with his approval.

In a letter to the Reverend James Somerville in Montreal, Fitz wrote: "This affair is much praised and the Americans think it a brilliant one on our part, but for myself it is an evidence most convincing of the deficiency of our officers in general." What infuriated Fitz was that the officers gave their position away by shouting before they had formed their line to attack.

> Never was surprise more complete — never was anything more
> brilliant than it would have been had we kept silence and not fired,
> but our officers began that which they should have watched with

The towering monument at Stoney Creek was erected by the Wentworth Women's Historical Society and unveiled by Queen Mary on June 6, 1913.

Gord Mallory.

Gord Mallory.

FitzGibbon's name is carved into one side of the Stoney Creek monument.

all their care to prevent; for they ought to have known that in darkness and noise confusion must be inevitable. I think I could have killed some of them had I been near them at the moment.[2]

Already, in his mind, Fitz was developing guerrilla tactics. Fighting in the woods of Canada called for stealth and cunning. He admired and emulated the Natives and militiamen, like Merritt, who knew the terrain and used that knowledge to outwit the Americans. Fitz felt a stronger bond to them than to his British superiors — he was fed up with procrastination and traditional methods of defence and attack. He desperately wanted to do something decisive.

In his first major battle at Egmont-op-Zee in Holland, Fitz had concluded that the best place to be in any battle was out in front. That day he had watched a brother of Isaac Brock lead his men from one sand hill to another, always in front in the thick of enemy fire. "After witnessing Savery Brock's conduct, I determined to be the first to advance every time at the head of those around me, and I soon saw that of those who were most prompt to follow me, fewer fell by the enemy's fire than I witnessed falling of those more in our rear."

What if he had 50 men to command in advance, to use in the woods as he saw fit? He went to Lieutenant-Colonel Harvey with his idea. Harvey told him to be back within an hour with a detailed plan of operation, which Harvey would take to General Vincent. Vincent, probably persuaded by Harvey, approved.

According to Fitz's granddaughter, the whole 49th Regiment wanted to join FitzGibbon's band. She quotes an old 49th man, who wrote in 1860, "We all wanted to go. We knew there would be good work, fighting and success wherever FitzGibbon led, for though impulsive he was prompt, and as brave as a lion. Through apparently foolhardy, every man in the regiment knew that he knew what he was about, and forgot nothing."[3]

Ensign Winder was Fitz's first choice. The other 48 rank and file came from the different companies of the 49th. Each man was already a "Green Tiger" in the jargon of the army, although this nickname was most often used by Americans to describe their fear of the 49ers. In battle after battle "those damned Green Tigers" would charge them with bayonets or storm their guns. Usually in the front of any fight, they were often the irresistible force that broke and scattered the blue American line. With 50 hand-picked men organized into a fast-moving, horse-riding band of holy terrors, the name Green Tiger would take on a new menace and many an American would wish he had never crossed the Niagara frontier.

Somewhere, FitzGibbon managed to get enough cloth to have 50 grey jackets made, as well as 50 red ones; the grey ones were camouflage ("Grey, being the nearest to the colour of the bark on the forest trees, is least discernible"). Sometimes he would use the jackets alternately to make it look like he had twice his numbers.

He divided his men into three parties, each in the charge of a sergeant, and began moving them, not by main roads, but by Native paths and escarpment trails, into territory where American raiding parties were robbing the farmers, terrorizing their wives, and taking old men prisoners. Fitz's assignment was to stop these assaults. He was also to collect information on the enemy's movements and do everything in his power to annoy the American Army.

Working with him was William Hamilton Merritt and his Provincial Dragoons. A group of them under Cornet McKenney were attached directly to FitzGibbon's party. British soldier and militiaman alike were delighted to be pushing again toward Fort George.

Lieutenant-Colonel Harvey, in a letter from Forty Mile Creek, June 11, 1813, explained Vincent's plan for the Niagara frontier and expressed the general's new admiration for the militia and yeomanry. (Harvey probably deserves credit for the better liaison and understanding between British officer and Niagara farmer.)

> The principal objects General Vincent has had in view in making a forward movement with the greatest part of the troops to this place are to communicate and give every support and assistance in his power to Sir James Yeo and the fleet and be at hand to take advantage of the success which we sanguinely anticipate from the approaching encounter with Commodore Chauncey, to give encouragement to the militia and yeomanry of the country, who are everywhere rising upon the fugitive Americans and making them prisoners, and withholding all supplies from them, and lastly (and perhaps chiefly) for the purpose of sparing the resources of the country in our rear and drawing the supplies of this army, as long as possible, from the country in the enemy's vicinity. Our position here secures all these important objects, and so long as our fleet is triumphant it is a secure one. Should any disaster (which God forbid) befall that we have no longer any business here or in this part of Canada.[4]

If Sir James Yeo could handle Chauncey on the water, the British Army, with men like Fitz and Merritt out in front, could pin the Americans inside Fort George. They might have to do it barefoot and half-clad, substituting a lot of spirit for a lack of supplies. On June 14, Vincent wrote to Colonel Baynes again about shoes, "I have to request shoes may be sent. We are more in want of them than any other article." On June 18, Captain James P. Fulton wrote to Sir George Prevost that he found the troops in great distress for shirts, shoes, and stockings, with most of the 49th "*literally* naked."

The food situation was also becoming dire. On June 10, Vincent sent all women and children belonging to the corps in Upper Canada to Montreal by bateaux. No rations were to be issued to soldiers' wives unless they were to serve as nurses. Sir James Yeo made a foray to the mouth of the Genesee River and captured all the provisions found in the government stores as well as a sloop laden with grain. This would help, but Vincent knew that all the rich resources of the Niagara Peninsula must be regained to keep his army fed.

By June 16, FitzGibbon was perched in a bold position at DeCew's, 11 kilometres inland from the army's advance post at the mouth of the Twelve Mile Creek, where Major De Haren was in command with 200 of the 104th Regiment and 300 Caughnawagas newly arrived from Lower Canada. Colonel Cecil Bisshopp waited at Twenty Mile Creek with a larger force. Vincent, with the main body of the British Army, was back at Forty Mile Creek. The DeCew position put Fitz at the point of a triangle, 11 kilometres from Major De Haren and 16 kilometres from Colonel Bisshopp. It was an ideal spot from which to swoop out in any direction; in particular, to take the Mountain Road through St. David's to Queenston and intercept the communication between Fort George and Fort Erie.

Dr. Cyrenius Chapin was the most hated man on the Niagara frontier. He led a troop of mounted men who swooped down on Niagara farmers, taking prisoners and plundering property. A doctor from Buffalo, he thought he was saving the Canadian settlers from British tyranny, but Fitz and his men were determined to save the settlers from the terror of Chapin.

Dr. Cyrenius Chapin

Dr. Cyrenius Chapin, a New England surgeon who moved to Buffalo in 1805, became notorious during the War of 1812. He led a band of horseback riders, who crossed the river to pillage homes and make settlers their prisoners.

With patients on both sides of the Niagara River, he had convinced himself that those on the Canadian side would be happy to join the United States. A few Canadians agreed with him; a group calling themselves Canadian Volunteers, led by Joseph Willcocks, who had served in the House of Assembly before turning against the government, often joined Chapin's marauders.

Chapin is the man who will guide an American expedition in an attempt to wipe out FitzGibbon at DeCew's.

Fitz's granddaughter tells a story that demonstrates the quick, calculated thinking and wild sense of humour that made him suited to this type of warfare. On one of his forays into the woods, he and two men met 10 or 12 Americans almost head-on. An overhanging bank of earth with a tangle of wild vines gave them a hiding place in the nick of time. The Americans had been following a path that ended on the top of the bluff and were unsure which way to go. FitzGibbon signalled his men to remain still; they watched Fitz creep along the bank toward a cave they knew about. A large fallen tree blocked the cave's entrance. The men saw him use his hand to pivot himself silently over the tree, at the same time getting a look at the enemy above him. Then an incredible bedlam of Native war whoops and wild Irish yells broke loose. Fitz was using the reverberations in the cave to sound like a horde of Natives and a pack of Green Tigers. Terrified, believing themselves ambushed, the Americans turned and fled. The two men under the vines could hear feet pounding on the path above them. They added some wild cries to the banshee voices of their leader and then, as Fitz emerged from the cave, his face lit up with glee, all three dissolved into well-earned laughter.

DeCew's House

John DeCew arrived in Upper Canada in 1787, a young man in a loyalist family. He found work as a surveyor, which helped him choose and acquire a mill site on a small creek flowing over the escarpment into Twelve Mile Creek. He claimed he paid an axe and a Native blanket for 100 acres. Later, a gold doubloon bought him another 100 acres.

In 1792, he built his sawmill and log cabin on Beaver Dams Creek. By 1808, the sawmill was prospering with a grist mill and linseed-oil operation added, and he was able to build a grand house with large fireplaces and walls finished in black walnut.

During the war, DeCew was an officer in the King's Militia in command of the 2nd Lincoln Militia. On May 29, 1813, after the Fort George battle, he was captured by the Americans as his regiment retreated.

Vincent wrote that he had established a depot of ammunition and provisions in a stone house belonging to a militia captain in a commanding position near the Beaver Dams. This impressive Georgian-style house on the edge of the escarpment, with its sweeping views and flourishing fruit trees, became FitzGibbon's headquarters, an oasis of civilization in the chaos of war. The grist mill was still operating, providing flour for the army. Army supplies were stored in the buildings. Mrs. DeCew and her children crowded into the upstairs rooms of the house while Fitz's 50 men, when they had time to eat or sleep, used the downstairs. She was delighted to harbour these "wild Irishmen" who might stop Chapin's "vagabonds" and win her husband's freedom from his Philadelphia prison.

But it wasn't all a lark. The prolonged tension and lack of decent rest and food often wore them weary and gaunt. Merritt says that FitzGibbon never slept twice in the same place. Charles Askin, writing to his father, fur-trader John Askin, called Fitz "one of the most active and pleasing officers we have," and said that he was "flying about in such a manner that the enemy did not know where to find him."

Typical of the fast pace that Fitz kept up was a sortie made on June 21. With Merritt, McKenney, Cummings, and young Barnard, staff adjutant to Colonel Bisshopp, Fitz was sent to Point Abino on Lake Erie to bring back a Mr. Tyce

Horn (Haun), who was helping the enemy. The entire area from Chippawa to Fort Erie was in American hands. Chapin was in the area, having passed by an hour before. The party would have to consider the possibility of meeting the Americans on the river road when they returned. The weather turned cold and it started to rain. Rain continued all night. At 2:00 a.m. they reached Horn's house and surrounded it. They were so cold they could hardly dismount from their horses, but they managed to take Horn and one of Chapin's men prisoners and in spite of their chilled condition, started the long ride back.

Merritt claimed he was back at Twelve Mile Creek by 9:00 the next morning, and went on to Forty Mile Creek to make out muster rolls, etc. — he didn't say whether Fitz went home to DeCew's for a rest, or onto his next escapade.

— — —

That June, Fitz received the only wound of his career. He had been walking noiselessly through the bush and stopped a moment to lean against a tree. Suddenly, he felt the presence of another person and turned in time to see a man fire at him. He felt the ball strike him and he staggered, but seconds later he was chasing the man. The man fell, dropped his rifle, and Fitz grabbed him. Ensign Winder had heard the shot and came running up. They took the man prisoner.

For two days, FitzGibbon was bruised, stiff, and sore. The prisoner was heard to tell people no bullet would kill "that damned Green Tiger," for he had certainly hit him. Fitz began to wonder himself why he wasn't dead. He and Winder went back to look and found that the ball had gone through a young tree before hitting him. That, combined with the thickness of his coat and the fact that he had turned in the nick of time, probably saved his life.

Many years later, in a letter to his youngest son, James, who was receiving his first commission in the 24th Regiment, Fitz passed on "advice for his guidance in woody warfare," knowledge garnered from these day of bush fighting in 1813 and 1814. "The troops should be drilled in the woods. The soldier, when advancing, should not go straight forward, but at an angle to some tree to the right or left of the one he quits." In the same letter, Fitz's admiration for the skill of the Natives was evident:

> I recommend that an intelligent Native be attached to each regiment for a sufficient time to teach all his lessons … to the officers and sergeants … One of the most efficient means of winning the highest degree of the soldier's goodwill and confidence is by carefully keeping him out of every unnecessary danger, and often going yourself to reconnoitre, rather than to send another to do so.

The physical fitness of his soldiers also concerned Fitz. "Let them run races, jump, leap, wrestle, use the pike, sword, stick, cricket-bat, quoits, as each may desire or you direct. Swimming should also be practised." Another of his favourite themes was fighting at night. "I think fighting at night has never been practised to one-tenth of the extent to which it is possible to carry it out." Speaking proudly of his band in 1813, he wrote, "I had men who could rejoice in being able to accomplish what other men would not think of even attempting."

Above all, an officer needed to have "knowledge of the comparative qualities of those he commands and those to whom he is opposed." Fitz saw two opposing armies as possessing "a certain quantum of courage and confidence, usually unequally divided and always liable to fluctuation." It was up to an officer "to so play his game that he shall from day to day and from one affair to another win from his adversary's scales more or less of these qualities, and transfer the gain to his own scales."[5] This was the distillation of his learning and experience, but in the summer of 1813, Fitz was still in the school of very hard knocks.

By June 20, he and Chapin were determined to get at each other. Fitz knew that Chapin, who did most of his raiding from Fort Erie to Chippawa, was in the area of Fort George. Several Green Tigers dispersed through the woods to locate him, while others removed the planks from the Chippawa Bridge to keep Chapin's 49 men from fleeing home to Buffalo when they closed in on him. The Green Tigers thought they had him, until it was discovered that 150

American infantrymen from Fort Erie had come over the bridge before they removed the planks.

Fitz had his men gathered in Lundy's Lane, ready to ambush Chapin's men at Forsyth's woods near the Falls. He had gone on ahead into the small village to reconnoitre, when a Mrs. Kirby, who lived on the corner, ran out waving at him to go back.

"There are two or three hundred men with Chapin and they just this moment passed by. For goodness sake," she pleaded, "go back!"

Fitz should have taken her advice, but he had spied an American horse by Deffield's Inn and, assuming there was only one American inside, decided he could take him. He rode over, dismounted, and entered the inn, where he found not one American but two, a rifleman and a soldier. Fitz soon had a rifle pointed at him. He summoned all his Irish charm and pretended to be an old acquaintance. This put the Americans off their guard for an instant. Merritt said Fitz proffered one hand in greeting and, with the other, seized the rifle.

> The soldier was in the act of firing when he fortunately caught his gun, brought both of them under his arm, by which means the muzzles of each were pointing at his comrade, both cocked, the friction of the two enabled him to keep them so firm that they could not with every exertion break his grasp. In this position he pulled and pushed them both out of the house, the steps of which were two or three feet high, he swearing and demanding them to surrender, they retorting the demand on him.

The *Montreal Gazette*, which had discovered that the doings of FitzGibbon's little band made good reading, got the story three weeks later and told it this way:

> In this situation Lieut. F. called upon two men who were looking on to assist him in disarming the two Americans, but they would not interfere. Poor Mrs. Kirby, apparently distracted, used

Gord Mallory.

These fireplaces and the foundation are all that remain of John DeCew's beautiful house, once a haven for Fitz and his Green Tigers.

all her influence, but in vain. The rifleman finding that he could not disengage his piece, drew Lieut. F.'s sword out of his scabbard with his left hand with the intention of striking at Lieut. F., when another woman, Mrs. Danfield [Deffield?], seized the uplifted arm and wrested the sword from his grasp. At this moment an elderly man, named Johnson, came up and forced the American from his hold on the rifle, and Lieut. F. immediately laid the other soldier prostrate.[6]

Merritt said Fitz got on his horse, led the other horse, and drove the two gentlemen before him to his party. "He had not left the place two minutes before the [American] party returned. Upon the whole it was a most gallant, daring and miraculous proceeding."

Whenever Fitz had to talk about such incidents he said he had been plain foolish. But miraculously, he had got away with them all. Tiger was an apt name to describe him. He was a cat with nine lives, nimble, lithe, quick, and cool — not yet a hero but about to become one.

He and Dr. Cyrenius Chapin were about to meet at Beaver Dams, where he would stake one of his nine lives and win fame and promotion at the Battle of Beaver Dams. At the same time, a woman named Laura Secord would gain immortal fame.

CHAPTER 8
LAURA SECORD'S LONG WALK

And when the Yankees did surrender, we all wondered what the mischief he [FitzGibbon] would do with them.
— Judge Jarvis of Brockville, with FitzGibbon at Beaver Dams[1]

The Battle of Stoney Creek drastically changed the chess pieces in this war. The British were no longer on the run. The Americans, who had briefly been in command of the whole Niagara frontier, with Chauncey protecting them on the water, sighted Sir James Yeo on the water and scurried back to Fort George, pulling in their troops from Fort Erie and virtually trapping themselves in the fort.

When they tried to break out, a woman walked 32 kilometres to warn James FitzGibbon that the Americans were coming to get him. That walk made Laura Secord a Canadian legend. As with all legends, facts have been altered and embellished. Someone put a cow in the story and it has been hard to get out. Then the woman herself, clad in lacy bonnet, became forever associated with a delicious brand of chocolates, giving the story a special flavour.

James and Laura Secord's house sat under the shadow of Queenston Heights. Portage (River) Road came down the Heights, running close to the Secord house, and along it clattered all the "going and coming" of whichever army held Fort George. The windows of the house looked toward the Niagara River and the Queenston

Wharf, where the Americans landed in October 1812. On that October day when General Brock died on the Heights above Laura's home, her husband James, a sergeant in the 1st Lincoln Militia, had been badly wounded in the shoulder and knee. Laura herself had gone to the Heights, searched among the dying for her husband, and with the help of "a Gentleman" got him down the hill into their own house.

She returned home to find her house a wreck, plundered by the Americans. Laura swallowed her tears and anger as she made her husband a bed in a corner of the chaos. She took James and their children to spend the winter with relatives in St. David's, five kilometres west of Queenston. In June 1813, Queenston was still at the mercy of the Americans, and James was still unwell from the wounds in his shoulder and knee, but the Secords were back at their own hearth. Portage Road was an American thoroughfare these days, although it made James grin with pride to see FitzGibbon's or Merritt's horsemen dash along it now and again on some surreptitious errand.

Laura never knew when Americans would knock on her door and demand lodging or food. When they did she had to comply. Although she never put in writing exactly how she learned of the plan to capture FitzGibbon, legend and her grandchildren agree that American soldiers taking food in her home revealed the scheme. Her granddaughter, Laura Secord Clark, says that Laura gave them food and liquor, then listened outside the window.

Cyrenius Chapin started the agitation to "get FitzGibbon." He and Fitz had been playing cat and mouse for over a month, and Chapin had a scheme to decide finally who was the cat. While Fitz and his friends were riding to Point Abino to capture Tyce Horn, Chapin was on his way to Fort George with his plan. He would convince Lieutenant-Colonel Boerstler that he had spied out the route to DeCew's, and could guide Boerstler there with 500 men, taking out the 50 British and close to 100 Natives there with ease.

On that wet and unseasonably cold June 21, it's possible that Chapin and his men would have stopped at the Secord house before riding on to Fort George. It is easy to picture them, warmed by food and drink, leaning back in their chairs to boast about getting those Green Tigers.

Laura often heard of FitzGibbon from her half-brother, Charles Ingersoll, a lieutenant in Merritt's Niagara Provincial Light Dragoons. She knew that without his band and Merritt's Dragoons they would be entirely under the American thumb. When the Americans had gone, she told her husband what she had heard, and added, "Somebody has to warn FitzGibbon." Her crippled husband remarked wryly that if he crawled on his hands and knees he could not get there in time. Laura thought of Chapin at Fort George preparing to ambush the men at DeCew's. She had no idea how quickly the force might move out. She made her decision. She herself would go.

At Fort George, Chapin was having his problems. Lieutenant-Colonel Charles Boerstler had no respect for the doctor turned highwayman. He did have a healthy respect for the British Army and for Lieutenant FitzGibbon's Green Tigers. He was not at all convinced that Chapin knew the roads, trails, swamps, and the British positions well enough to get him to DeCew's and back alive. But it seems that Chapin got through to a higher authority, Brigadier-General John P. Boyd, the American officer in charge at Fort George. On June 23, Boyd gave Charles Boerstler orders to take 500 men to DeCew's house and capture or wipe out the enemy stationed there. He was to march his men to Queenston in the evening and, with Chapin leading, reach DeCew's the following day. Boerstler was shocked, but he got the operation under way.

Meanwhile, Laura had left the house at 4:30 in the morning on June 22. As the story is told by FitzGibbon's granddaughter, Laura pretended to be trying to catch a cow to milk it when an American sentry questioned her. But Laura's biographer, Ruth Mackenzie, says there was no cow and probably no sentry either. Anyway, Laura had another excuse for being abroad so early. She would tell any American she met that she was on her way to visit her brother, Charles, lying sick of a fever at Hannah Secord's house near St. David's. (Charles was engaged to marry Hannah's daughter, Elizabeth.)

Charles was still sick in bed. Laura may have hoped that he would help her with the message but he was unable to get up. Elizabeth Secord offered to go with Laura and the two women set out. Afraid of American patrols on the Mountain Road to Beaver Dams, they took the Old Swamp Road west to Shipman's

Corners (St. Catharines), then turned south to DeCew's. This way led over miry roads made worse by the all-night rain, through sloughs and muddy swamp that tugged at their feet and slowed their pace. They were often in the shadow of deep woods where mosquitoes rose in clouds to add to their misery. When not in the shade of trees, the day was becoming excessively hot.

At Shipman's Corners, Elizabeth could go no farther; she would stay at the home of a friend. She was unwell and had only a year to live. Laura, although she

Natives in the War of 1812

Tecumseh had 600 Natives with him when Brock captured Fort Detroit, but after that success as many as 3,000 Natives from many tribes aligned themselves with the British.

Mohawks on the Niagara Peninsula joined the British to defend home territory. In 1784, most of their lands in New York State had been lost to the American Revolution. Many of them moved north and were granted six miles on either side of the Grand River by the British government. In time, they would lose much of that land to White settlers and the remaining tract would become the Six Nations Indian Reserve.

Mohawks belong to the Six Nations League of Peace, or Iroquois Confederacy. This early experiment in democracy, with its council of 50 chiefs elected by female elders, would be copied by the governments of both the United States and the United Nations. Originally, five tribes made up the confederacy — Mohawk, Oneida, Seneca, Cayuga, and Onondaga. Tuscarora were admitted later. Mohawks who still lived in New York State were determined to remain neutral in the war.

At Queenston Heights, Mohawks, led by Chief John Brant, played a decisive role in pushing the wave of Americans back from the Heights to the river.

In June 1813, 180 Caughnawagas, under Dominique Ducharme, arrived from Lower Canada just in time for the Battle of Beaver Dams. Caughnawagas were Iroquois (mostly Mohawk and Oneida) who adopted the Catholic religion and separated from the Confederacy in the second half of the 17th century. They were sometimes referred to as "French Praying Indians." Although there were 200 regular Mohawks and some western Natives at Beaver Dams, Caughnawagas did the fighting. John

looked frail, was strong and tough. But as she went on alone, she was afraid. Every woman she had encountered along the way had warned her of the Natives. There were hundreds of them encamped in the woods, they had said, and no woman was safe among them. Laura, marching on, told herself the Natives were friends to the British and the stories of their atrocities much exaggerated. If only she'd known the territory better — the hills, ravines, and passes through the valleys confused her, and she kept taking the wrong trails. It was uphill, too, as she was actually

Norton, war chief of the Mohawks, summed up the situation: "The Cognawaga *[sic]* Indians *fought the* battle, *the* Mohawks *or Six Nations got the* plunder, *and* FitzGibbon *got the* credit."[2]

Years later, in 1818, FitzGibbon put his testimony on paper:

> *With respect to the affair with Captain Boerstler, not a shot was fired on our side by any but the Indians. They beat the American detachment into a state of terror, and the only share I claim is taking advantage of a favourable moment to offer them protection from the tomahawk and scalping knife. The Indian department did all the rest.[3]*

John Norton's Mohawks played a major role in keeping the Americans imprisoned in Fort George that summer. Working with the Mohawks were smaller numbers of Delaware, Ottawa, Chippawa, and Mississauga.

When Tecumseh died that September, only 700 of his Natives followed Procter back to Burlington Heights. These disheartened Natives played little part in the remaining battles. Many returned to Ohio territory. Caughnawagas would fight again in the remaining battles of war, at Châteauguay and Chrysler's Farm.

At the beginning of July, when the British attacked Black Rock, neutral New York Seneca decided to strike back. The result was members of the Confederacy fighting against each other at the Battle of Chippawa later that month. Eighty of them were killed. After this battle the Grand River Mohawks withdrew from the fighting to save their confederacy.

climbing the escarpment. The day was wearing on to the edge of darkness. She was almost too tired to think, too exhausted to walk. Suddenly, she found herself surrounded by Natives.

All the sensible things she had kept telling herself about the Natives gave way to complete terror and she could not speak. But the authority of their chief in quieting the others reassured her. She was able to make him understand that the Americans were coming, that she had to talk to FitzGibbon. Finally, the chief volunteered to go with her to DeCew's house.

When they arrived, James FitzGibbon was more than a little surprised to hear the story of this frail little woman who claimed to have walked from Queenston. Queenston was 32 kilometres distant by the Old Swamp Road. But her obvious fatigue, her bedraggled appearance, and the urgency in her voice made it impossible to doubt her. Native scouts may have already alerted Fitz that the Americans were on the move. What Laura had heard confirmed it.

"Mrs. Secord," he wrote later, "was a person of slight and delicate frame and made this effort in weather excessively warm, and I dreaded at the time that she must suffer in health in consequence of fatigue and anxiety, she having been exposed to danger from the enemy, through whose line of communication she had to pass."[4]

FitzGibbon sent her to Turney's farm at the Crossroads beyond DeCew's where, as she expressed it later, she "slept right off."

Fitz could not tell how much time he had. He sent a message to Colonel Bisshopp and Major De Haren but knew he might have to act without them. There were 400 Natives at the Beaver Dams, about three kilometres east of DeCew's house. One hundred eighty of them were Caughnawagas, newly arrived from Lower Canada under a militia captain, Dominique Ducharme. Captain William Kerr commanded 200 from the Six Nations, mostly Mohawks, and 80 men from various other tribes. By nightfall, Kerr had the Natives posted in good position to intercept the Americans and he stayed on guard during the night. In the morning, he sent Captain Ducharme to reconnoitre. Ducharme went all the way to the Niagara River, got into a battle with a small party of Americans, killed four and took seven prisoners. But he saw no sign of 500 marching men.

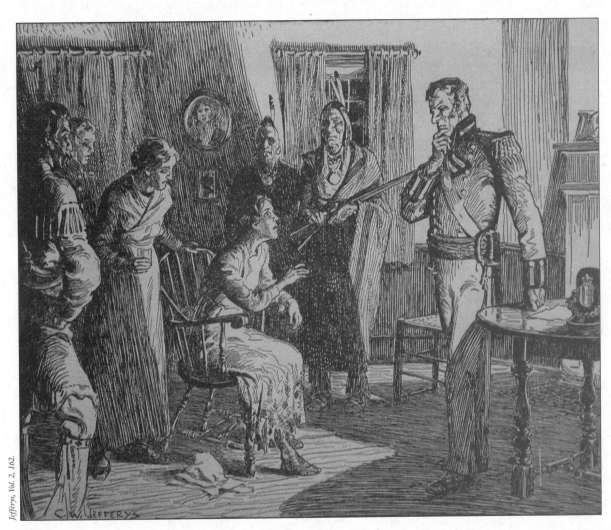

Jefferys, Vol. 2, 162.

Laura Secord is delivering her message to Captain FitzGibbon at DeCew's.

On the following morning, June 24, Ducharme's scouts did discover the Americans on the move. Boerstler's little army had spent the night in Queenston, throwing out patrols and pickets to prevent any citizen carrying the news. Early the next morning they marched out, confident that surprise was on their side.

The Americans were near their destination, hot and weary from the march, when the beechwoods on either side of them exploded with savage yells and rifle fire. Cavalrymen riding rearguard fell from their horses. Natives appeared on the road behind them, cutting off the possibility of retreat. Near the front of the long column, Colonel Boerstler was shot in the thigh. Major Taylor, second-in-command, had his horse shot from under him. Captain Chapin ran to hide behind the ammunition wagons, to the intense fury of Boerstler. Not only had Chapin forced him into this desperate attempt, he had admitted en route that he did not know the roads so that Boerstler had to force a settler to guide his troops; now Cyrenius Chapin was hiding from the enemy.

The fire from the woods was incessant — the Americans could find no escape from it. They attempted to charge the Natives to drive them into an open field, but Boerstler found his men were not equal to the Natives in woodland warfare, and they had to fall back. FitzGibbon, who had watched from a high hill to the right of the road, kept careful calculation of the despair and panic in the American ranks. When he thought the moment was right, he rode up with a white handkerchief tied to his sword, while his bugler sounded a ceasefire to the Natives. The beechwoods became still.

Fitz had bluffed his way out of tricky situations before, but these were higher odds than he usually played. Could he make 500 regular soldiers surrender to his 50 Green Tigers and some Natives they could not see?

British reinforcements had arrived, Fitz said (wishing it was true), and the Natives were becoming hard to control, especially the western ones. In order to avoid bloodshed he must urge the Americans to surrender. Boerstler said he would not surrender to a force he had not even seen. Fitz swallowed hard and said he would ask his superior officer if he might allow one of Boerstler's officers to inspect the British troops.

Fitz did not have any "superior officer." The only British troops he had, apart from his own Green Tigers, were 20 Dragoons who had galloped up under Captain Hall of Chippawa. Maybe Hall would do. "You be my superior officer," he told Hall, "receive the request and refuse it."

Boerstler sent Lieutenant Goodwin to Hall, who refused the "humiliation" of having his troops inspected. Next, Boerstler sent Captain McDowell to ask that he be given until sundown to decide on surrender (it was then about noon).

FitzGibbons replied, "I cannot possibly grant such a request. I could not control the Natives for such a length of time. I cannot give your general more than five minutes in which to decide whether to surrender or not."

Boerstler's decision was to surrender. He was 27 kilometres from Fort George with no hope of reinforcements, and had no idea how many British troops or Natives opposed him. A 27-kilometre retreat with exhausted men at the mercy of the Natives was unthinkable. Fitz promised them protection from the Natives and personally spoke with each of the chiefs, extracting promises from them that they would not harm any Americans taken prisoner.

As FitzGibbon was about to accept the surrender of the troops, Major De Haren galloped up from Twenty Mile Creek, prepared to take over. FitzGibbon's Irish temper flared. He knew the prize he had, and he had worked too hard for the British cause to have his glory snatched away. In an age when officers were usually wealthy men who could afford to purchase their commissions (Isaac Brock had paid $15,000 to rise from ensign to lieutenant-colonel in 13 years) James FitzGibbon had gone into debt to buy his commission as ensign in 1806 and not been out of debt since. Promotion would mean increased pay as well as a chance to rise farther in the ranks. He needed both.

Grabbing De Haren's horse, Fitz said in an emphatic whisper, "Not another word, sir, not another word; these men are my prisoners." Stepping back, he asked, "Shall I proceed to disarm the American troops?"

De Haren answered, "You may."

Fitz formed the Americans in file to keep their ranks broken, fearing De Haren might reveal the scarcity of British troops. (He doesn't say how far away

Laura Secord's monument is at Queenston Heights, not far from her house.

Gord Mallory.

De Haren's companies were but they had not yet put in an appearance.) Keeping the Americans apart from his handful of British soldiers, Fitz asked De Haren, "Shall the American troops ground their arms here?"

"No, let them march through between our men and ground their arms on the other side."

Fitz turned a wicked glare on De Haren. Did the man not realize that with a close look at their tiny British force, the Americans might not ground their arms

Gord Mallory.

Laura's image has appeared on thousands of chocolate boxes — this one is from the 1940s.

at all? In desperation, he said, "Do you think it prudent to march them through with arms in their hands in the presence of the Indians?"

Boerstler saved the day for FitzGibbon. "For God's sake, sir," he exclaimed, "do what this officer bids you."

"Do so," said De Haren.

But the moment the American soldiers put down their arms, Natives sprang forward. The terrified men began to seize their arms again. Fitz jumped upon a tree stump and shouted, "Americans, don't touch your arms! Not a hair on your head shall be hurt. Remember, I am here." A bombastic speech, he admitted afterward, but the chiefs had given him their promise and he believed them. The Natives helped themselves to pistols, swords, and jackets that pleased them, contrary to the terms of capitulation, but none of them inflicted physical harm. At last, Fitz could relax. De Haren requested that Fitz conduct Colonel Boerstler to DeCew's house.

Laura Secord's Legacy and the Chocolate Connection

In a certificate written in 1827, James FitzGibbon spoke of how much he (and indirectly we) owed to Laura Secord, saying that he had ever held himself personally indebted to her.

Laura was born in Massachusetts and came to Canada with her Loyalist family in 1795. In 1797, she married James Secord, another Loyalist, son of an officer in Butler's Rangers. James, fighting with the militia, helped to carry Isaac Brock's body from the field of battle on the morning of October 13, 1812.

Laura's 32-kilometres walk received little recognition in her lifetime. In 1860, the Prince of Wales (later Edward VIII) visited Niagara Falls, heard her story, and awarded her a gift of $100. She was 85 years old at the time. She died in 1868, at 93. Her grave marker in Drummond Hill Cemetery tells the story of her walk.

In 1901, a monument to Laura was placed on Queenston Heights. In 1971, her homestead at 29 Queenston Street was restored and is now a museum portraying life in 1812.

In 1913, a chocolate company helped to make Laura famous when they named their candy after her. Their first store opened in Toronto. If she was not already a Canadian icon, she became one on the chocolate boxes.

After 1999, the production of Laura Secord chocolates was moved to Chicago, although the chocolate was still made in Canada. In 2011, the Laura Secord brand came home to Canada when Nutriart, a Quebec company, bought its 125 Canadian stores.

As they rode the three kilometres together, FitzGibbon discovered he liked Boerstler. The wound in his leg looked painful but he rode without complaining. He had been caught in a vicious trap, the victim of poor planning by his superior officers, poor guidance by Chapin, and the courage of a woman whose long walk FitzGibbon would keep secret to protect her throughout the remainder of the war.

Colonel Boerstler would go home to face a court of enquiry but its final verdict would be that his personal deportment "was that of a brave, zealous and deliberate officer, and the conduct of the regular officers and men under his command was equally honourable to themselves and to their country."[5]

Chapin was a prisoner of the British at last, but he proved a hard man to hold. On July 12, he and 25 of his men were sent east to Kingston under a guard of sixteen soldiers in two boats. At a signal from Chapin, his men in the second boat drew alongside and boarded the boat Chapin was in. In the struggle, Chapin's men overpowered their guard, turned their boats back, and landed the next day at Fort George. Chapin kept his freedom until the end of December, when he was again taken prisoner at Buffalo; that time the British managed to convey him, with no mistakes, to a Quebec jail.

Meanwhile, FitzGibbon's performance caught the imagination of the Canadas and he became the "hero of Beaver Dams."

CHAPTER 9

FEVER, COLD RAIN, AND GRAND ATTACKS UPON THE ONIONS

We are placed in a strange situation, from being invaders of a territory we are now preparing to meet an attack from the invaded and our limits are so circumscribed that we scarcely hold enough of Canada to rest our wearied limbs upon.
— *New York Evening Post*, August 3, 1813. Extract of a letter to a gentleman in this city, dated Fort George, Upper Canada, July 20, 1813[1]

As a result of the battle at Beaver Dams, FitzGibbon was promoted to captain in the Glengarry Light Infantry Fencibles. However, he stayed with the 49th for the rest of the 1813 campaign. His promotion may have been due to both Boerstler's capture and his services with the Green Tigers. Baynes wrote to Prevost, recommending Fitz for his recent success but also for his distinguished service as an officer of a light corps. Vincent also wrote to Prevost pointing out that his actions brought about the surrender of the American attachment.

The *Montreal Gazette* relished Fitz's latest adventure. They had the story by the 6th of July: "We have much satisfaction in communicating to the public the particulars of a campaign not of a *General* with his *thousands* but of a *lieutenant* with his *tens* only." The story went on to talk of "the cool determination and the hardy presence of mind evinced by this highly meritorious officer," and to suggest that "the brilliant result which crowned these exertions will, while they make known to the world the name of Lieutenant FitzGibbon, reflect new lustre if possible, on the well-earned reputation of the gallant 49th Regt., and class that event with the most extraordinary occurrences of the present accursed war."[2]

The real significance of the affair was its effect on the Americans. President Madison ordered General Dearborn to resign shortly after the Boerstler fiasco, and the command of the army went to Generals Boyd and Lewis. For the rest of the summer, the Americans kept 4,000 men cooped up inside Fort George. James J. Fulton, aide-de-camp to Sir George Prevost, wrote on June 28, "Indeed, from anything we learn since Colonel Boerstler's disaster, they have not dared to send a patrol more than one mile from Fort George in any direction."

The British, infused with new spirit, pressed closer. At the end of June, Vincent moved his whole army (about 1,800 men) up to the Twelve Mile Creek. On the first of July the advanced posts of the army were pushed on to St. David's. Soldiers, militiamen, and Natives were all in a mood to take the offensive. No one was more eager to get on with the action than Captain Fitz. On July 4, he had Ensign Winder organize a party of seven Green Tigers, 34 militiamen, and one volunteer to cross the Niagara in three boats and attack Fort Schlosser, opposite Chippawa. It was the night of Independence Day and FitzGibbon had calculated to catch the Americans off guard. Winder took the guard by surprise and, in less than one hour, came away with a gunboat, two bateaux, anchors, 120 barrels of salt, eight barrels of pork, whiskey, and tobacco. No one on either side was hurt.

Fitz had intended a simultaneous raid on Black Rock, an important post opposite Fort Erie, downriver from Buffalo. Black Rock would be heavily guarded so he had reserved the rest of his band for this attack. But it proved impossible to get enough boats for his 40 men, so he had to postpone the raid.

A few days later, Lieutenant-Colonel Bisshopp went to FitzGibbon with another plan to attack Black Rock. Fitz had his men hidden in barns near Fort Erie and was watching the enemy with a spyglass when Bisshopp and two other redcoats walked up in full view of the enemy, to FitzGibbon's great disgust. The Americans were not aware that the British had moved so close to the frontier, and he had been planning a perfect surprise for them. Bisshopp said he was trying to collect 300 men for the raid, but could only obtain 200. Did FitzGibbon think the place could be taken with so few men? Fitz grinned and said he was ready to take it with 44 as soon as he had boats. He had already ordered Winder to bring the four bateaux from Chippawa.

"Oh, then, I need ask you no more questions, but go and bring the two hundred men."

Bisshopp had his men there the following day with enough boats to make the crossing. Fitz would lead the advance and cover the retreat should they be attacked.

"At two the following morning we moved off. My men, being select and good boatmen, soon gained the opposite shore, but owing to the strength of the current and the boats being filled with men, further down than we intended."[3] Fitz saw that the boats behind him would be driven even farther down and would be a good half-hour later in landing than his own men. He could see 150 armed enemy militiamen emerging from the barracks to meet them. It looked as if he would have to stage a show and stall for time.

There was always a good measure of comedy when Fitz was called upon to act, and this was no exception. There was mist over the river, and he depended on it to camouflage and, he hoped, magnify the numbers of his men while he advanced ahead of them with his bugler and his flag of truce to meet the American commander, Major Hall.

Mary Agnes FitzGibbons says he met the militiamen with these words: "I see you are all militia, and I do not wish to be killing the husbands, fathers and brothers of your innocent families. You shall all be allowed to retire on parole."

Before he could finish his speech, the militia ranks had broken, and the men were running down the hill to Buffalo as fast as they could go. "Stop your men, Major Hall," Fitz called out, hardly able to keep from laughing. "This is quite irregular while negotiating under a flag of truce."

"I know it, sir," replied the indignant American officer, "but I cannot stop them."[4]

By the time Bisshopp arrived, FitzGibbon had dismissed Major Hall, who had gone down the hill after his men. The coast was clear for the work to be done. They seized eight large boats into which they put two 12-pounders, one 6-pounder, and a large quantity of military stores and provisions. Half their men were detached to get these stores away. The other half went to burn the block-house, barracks that could hold 5,000 men, and a schooner anchored there.

But the party lasted too long. According to Mary Agnes, her grandfather wanted to get away but Colonel Bisshopp had his eye on 400 barrels of salt down the beach. Meanwhile, the burning buildings revealed their numbers to the American militia, by then strengthened by a force from Buffalo and a number of Seneca Natives. They made a furious attack on the hundred-odd British who remained on shore. Driven to their boats, the British left behind a captain and 15 men killed or wounded. Another 27 killed or wounded were in the boats. Someone cried that Colonel Bisshopp was wounded and had been left ashore. A boatload of Green Tigers made a rush for him and got him into their boat, where he was wounded twice more. He died five days later from the wounds.

About the experience, FitzGibbon wrote,

> For no man fallen in battle, did I grieve so much as for him. He was a man of most gentle and generous nature, and was more be-loved by the militia over whom he was an inspecting field officer, than any other who served in the province during the war. But he wanted either experience or judgement, and fell in consequence in the prime of life, in the twenty-eighth year of his age.[5]

Meanwhile, the new military commander for Upper Canada, Major-General Francis Baron de Rottenburg, had arrived to take a larger look at the future of the war. In a letter to Sir George Prevost, written from Twelve Mile Creek, July 7, 1813, he described conditions as he saw them:

I am using every exertion to repair the roads. They have been much neglected by my predecessor and are the worst I ever saw anywhere....

That stronghold [Burlington Heights] I must retire to ultimately and maintain myself until the navy will be enabled to meet the fleet on Lake Ontario. Had Sir James Yeo time to spare to co-operate with the army, Fort George would have fallen. But I do not now possess means of attacking them on both sides of the river.

Lieut. FitzGibbon is a deserving and enterprising officer and I shall forward your letter to him. [Prevost had written to inform FitzGibbon of his promotion. Mary Agnes FitzGibbon says that letter was lost among his private papers.]

With the exception of Lieut-Colonel Harvey, who is a most active, zealous, and intelligent officer, the heads of the departments here are deficient in activity and cleverness, and the militia staff is most miserable. There is a vast deal to be done in this Province. Everything is unhinged and requires my utmost exertions to keep affairs in some shape or other.[6]

It seems de Rottenburg, like Vincent, did not achieve instant understanding with the militia. Merritt gives us a militiaman's reaction to him,

I was presented to Major-General de Rottenburg who had arrived to take the command of the army as well as being President of the Province. He unfortunately brought with him a very great name. We expected he would have performed wonders, in fact he has done nothing but eat, drink, snuff and snuffle.[7]

On July 20, de Rottenburg wrote to Sir George Prevost that he had moved to St. David's, "which reduces the enemy to the ground he stands upon and prevents his getting any supplies from our territory." He also mentioned that it had become

Major-General De Rottenburg

De Rottenburg, who was Swiss, served in the French Army, then joined the British in 1795. He served in Lower Canada in 1812 but in 1813, when Sheaffe was removed from command after losing York to the Americans, he replaced Sheaffe as military administrator of Upper Canada.

His performance was even less applauded than Sheaffe's. He was cautious and slow to move against the enemy. Major-General Henry Procter, commanding the western army, believed he could capture the American fleet at Presqu'ile if de Rottenburg would not, fearing that doing so would weaken the armies at Burlington Heights and Kingston. As Procter and de Rottenburg argued, Tecumseh's agitation increased.

After Procter's defeat, Canadian-born Gordon Drummond was named lieutenant-governor of Upper Canada and de Rottenburg was moved back to Lower Canada.

necessary to keep the Natives occupied, and that they were busy "harassing and teasing them the whole day long."[8]

The stalemate at Fort George for the rest of the summer was a direct result of the deadlock on Lake Ontario. Sir James Yeo had had some advantage when Chauncey was staying close to Sackets Harbor until his new ship, *General Pike*, would be ready to sail. Yeo had been able to support Vincent as he moved toward Fort George, and to conduct raids along the south shore of Lake Ontario. But on July 21, the new corvette *General Pike* led Chauncey's squadron out of Sackets Harbor.

The *General Pike*, with 26 long 24-pounders, had a greater range of fire than any British ship. Altogether, Chauncey had two ships, one brig, and 10 schooners, while Yeo's fleet consisted of two ships, two brigs, and two schooners. At Fort Niagara, Chauncey took on troops to attack Vincent's supply depot at Burlington Heights. But this post had been reinforced by Colonel Battersby, who had marched from York with part of the Glengarry corps. When Chauncey saw the

Gord Mallory.

From 2012 to 2014, these re-enactors will celebrate the 200th anniversary of the War of 1812.

Glengarries there he realized that York must be defenceless and decided instead to make another attack on York. On August 1, he landed his Americans, who burnt barracks and storehouses and carried away provisions, mainly flour.

On August 7, Yeo's fleet met Chauncey's off the Niagara River, and a decisive battle seemed inevitable. Instead, the two commanders manoeuvred all night. Around midnight a storm came up and two of Chauncey's schooners capsized and were lost. All but 13 of the men on board went down with the ships.

The two fleets danced around each other for five successive days. In the early hours of August 11, Chauncey's two best schooners became separated from the American fleet and were captured by Yeo. Finally, Chauncey sailed away to Sackets Harbor with four ships fewer than when he sailed out. Yeo had no desire to tangle with those long guns on the *General Pike*, but he could out sail the American fleet and occasionally he might cut out one of Chauncey's schooners. The rest of the time he would let Chauncey chase him around Lake Ontario, as the two fleets danced a sort of international ballet to the great disgust of land commanders on both sides.

In mid-August there was excitement in the ranks as Sir George Prevost arrived and ordered "general demonstration" on the morning of August 24. While the larger part of the army performed before Fort George, 350 men under Major Plenderleath crossed the river and crept through the woods to surprise the Americans manning the guns and batteries opposite Fort George. Included in this number was FitzGibbon's party of Green Tigers. Fourteen Americans were taken prisoner, the rest driven back to Fort Niagara. Three 49ers were wounded.

On the Canadian side, British soldiers were delighted to dash into the town beside Fort George. The Americans opened a brisk fire from house windows and garden walls but still the British were "extremely unwilling to come away." Colonel Harvey stopped at his old quarters to snatch up a box of valuables he had left there. With their pickets all taken prisoner, the American Army stayed inside Fort George. No amount of manoeuvring by Prevost's army could induce them to come out. In his dispatch afterward, Prevost said he was convinced that Fort George could not be taken without more troops, help from the fleet, and a battering train.

Gord Mallory.

The American line advances (re-enactors as they appeared in the battles of 1812–14).

Prevost went back to Kingston to try to convince Sir James Yeo to do something decisive on the water. The troops settled down to being sick. By the end of August the spirit had gone out of the soldiers on the Niagara frontier. Idleness and bad food bred misery as real and awful as the sufferings of battle. Sickness stalked in every camp, and by September 6, de Rottenburg wrote, "I have now in the rear at the Twelve Mile Creek and at York, five hundred men sick."

In a private letter to Sir George Prevost, sent on August 30, de Rottenburg said, "Colonels Stewart, Plenderleath, May, Williams, FitzGibbon, and a great number of others are laid up with the lake fever. We are in great want of medicine and wine for the sick."

Fitz was possibly cared for by one of his own Green Tigers who had recovered from or not caught the fever. He may have lain sick at DeCew's or he may have been conveyed to one of the crude hospitals set up at Twelve Mile Creek.

In his September 21 letter home, Thomas Ridout mentioned two officers who had died, then added, "FitzGibbon has got well again."

On September 19, Sir George Prevost wrote to Sir James Lucas Yeo:

> The Centre Division of the Upper Canada Army is placed in a situation very critical and one novel in the system of war, that of investing a force vastly superior in numbers within a strongly entrenched position. It was adopted and has been maintained from a confident expectation that with the squadron under your command a combined attack ere this could have been effected on the enemy at Fort George with every prospect of success. To the local disadvantages of the positions occupied by our army have been added disease and desertion to a degree calling for an immediate remedy.[9]

As inexperienced new troops arrived from Europe they had to learn from the militiamen how to make shelters, light a smudge against mosquitoes, and cook enough to eat. Lieutenant MacEwan of the Royal Scots wrote to his wife, "I now live by myself in an Indian house made of branches and leaves of trees, all that defends me from cold and heat."

But most of the militia could not make lean-to shelters to keep out rain; their clothing did not repel water and by this time their boots leaked. More than one regiment was in rags. Merritt's troop had been disbanded because his people were "literally naked and defenceless." Merritt himself was sent to Montreal to plead his need for appointments and better organization for his Dragoon force.

Sanitation and Sickness

The fierce cold of winter kept troops healthy; the lovely Canadian summer made them sick. At Niagara, 2,000 men were camped together in whatever shelter they could rig, their clothing worn to rags and their meat often rancid. Salt was essential to keep meat edible in hot weather. A raid on Fort Schlosser in July had netted them 120 barrels of salt. Again, it was barrels of salt that delayed the British too long at Black Rock. But by September, salt was running out.

Sanitation was poor or non-existent, resulting in diarrhoea and dysentery. In 1813, the dreaded "lake fever" (typhus) stalked the camps on both sides of the river. In Sackets Harbor at that time, one-fifth of the men had dysentery or jaundice or rheumatism or lake fever. With a great many dying, it was discovered that their bread was contaminated, made with lake water drawn near the drainage from the latrines. Their fellow Americans in Fort George were no better off. By August, 1,200 of them were sick.

Meanwhile, the British camp at Twelve Mile Creek had 500 lying sick in the crude hospital there. Conditions in the hospital were anything but healthy. Dr. "Tiger" Dunlop described the scene there in the summer of 1814. "The weather was intensely hot, the flies were in myriads and lighting on the wounds, deposited their eggs, so that maggots bred in a few hours, producing dreadful irritation."[10]

Later that summer, he described the camp before Fort Erie. He had expected tents but there were none. The Canadian militia knew how to make thatched wigwams from hemlock boughs, which actually kept out the rain. Soldiers arriving from Europe lived in wet misery until they learned. But Dunlop saw that the European soldiers had other skills. He watched them gather a haversack of wild herbs, add some flour, and make "a capital kettle of soup" while the Canadians scorched their rancid meat in the fire.

Rain fell for two weeks and sickness increased. When Brown's army attacked on September 17, disease was overshadowed by the new sufferings of the battle.

When it rained on the soldiers their fires went out. What food was available was wet. Rain turned the low ground on which they were camped into swamp. Sanitation was poor in dry weather — in wet, it became a horror and a hazard to health. Dysentery and fever spread misery among the men and so shattered their morale that some no longer dreaded being shot by a Yankee. Others looked across the Niagara and imagined greener fields. Maybe it rained less over there. Everyone imagined more freedom over there, whatever freedom was. Numbers of them deserted to find out. Others tried and failed and were shot. Some sulked and disobeyed and were flogged.

Days dragged on in idleness and lack of purpose while they camped beside an enemy that would not come out to fight. Food grew scarcer. Settlers now hated the sight of redcoats because the soldiers were driven to stealing their apples and potatoes and hay, and burning their rail fences.

Young Thomas Ridout from York had been appointed to the commissariat at Niagara in July. His letters home show quite plainly how thing were. He was posted at St. David's, then, at the beginning of September, moved to the lakeside where 2,000 troops were camped. A Mr. Thompson had let them into an old unused house on his property.

We made a straw bed on the floor. We collect balm in the garden for tea, and carry on an extensive robbery of peas, apples, onions, corn, carrots, etc; for we can get nothing but by stealing, excepting milk, which is carefully measured. Bread and butter is out of the question, and to-day we sent a dragoon to the Twelve-Mile Creek for these articles and G. to the cross-roads for beef, etc. ... The army is getting very sickly, forty or fifty men are sent to hospital every day.

September 16th: We burn rails, steal apples, pears and peaches at a great rate. Old Lion sometimes growls at the rails going so fast, but can't help himself. He thinks me the most innocent of the lot.

September 21st.: We are in the same state at the old house as ever. I carry on the foraging. To-night our dragoon is to make a grand attack upon the onions. [11]

What the British Army did not steal, the Natives did. In midsummer, General de Rottenburg had found it necessary to issue a District General Order: "The ready sale found for articles by the Natives having encouraged depredations by them, all officers and soldiers are forbidden to purchase anything from an Indian without permission." He announced at the same time that any soldier caught taking hay or burning fences would be tried by "drumhead court martial."

CHAPTER 10
WAR ON THE WATER

It is too true that our fleet on Lake Erie is taken, and Procter is left at Amherstburg without provisions, guns or men. Most of the cannon were mounted on board the ships.
— Thomas Ridout to his father at York, September 21, 1813[1]

On the western front, Procter's army was becoming desperate for supplies. A long winter faced them with all the western Natives and their families to be fed, and the season for sailing would soon close.

On the water, Captain Robert H. Barclay was equally desperate. The burning of York by the Americans had destroyed the naval stores and guns destined for his brigs under construction at Amherstburg. While the Americans were building two large ships in Presqu'ile Harbour, Barclay kept his tiny fleet stationed like guard dogs just outside the sandbar at the harbour entrance. Barclay knew the new ships could not sail over the sandbar unless they removed their cannon.

But on the 1st of August, Barclay had to sail to Long Point for provisions. The Americans risked all to get their ships out that day. Without cannon, they were completely vulnerable to Barclay's return. The story is that a public dinner given for Barclay by the citizens of Port Dover kept him away too long. When he got back, Commodore Perry's ships had just made their escape.

Naval action on Lake Ontario and Lake Erie was often a game of hide-and-seek, depending on which commodore felt bolder at the time.

C.W. JEFFERYS

Jefferys, Vol. 2, 168.

Captain Robert Heriot Barclay

Scottish-born Barclay joined the Royal Navy at age 11, in 1798. Serving with Nelson, he lost his left arm while attacking a French convoy.

He arrived in Canada on May 5, 1813, and took charge of the ships at Kingston. But when Commodore James Lucas Yeo arrived two weeks later, Barclay was superseded and offered command of the Lake Erie squadron. With the Niagara Peninsula in the clutches of the Americans, he and his officers and seamen had to travel overland to get to Amherstburg.

Now the race was on, Barclay building the Detroit *to augment his two small vessels, Perry constructing two brigs and getting several vessels moved up from Black Rock.*

When the two fleets met, Barclay suffered defeat. To add injury to insult, he received two wounds, one in the thigh and one in his only arm. After his defeat he had to appear at a court-martial still wrapped in bandages. The result however was high praise for "... the Judgement and Gallantry of Captain Barclay...."

Barclay had to flee to Amherstburg for the rest of the summer to await the completion of his brig, *Detroit*. By September he had given up hope of more reinforcements arriving for his fleet. Since he also had no hope of receiving guns for the *Detroit*, he and Procter took guns off the ramparts of Fort Malden for the new ship. Barclay, urged on by Prevost, decided he would have to go out to confront Perry's fleet.

That the Risk is very great I feel very much, but that in the present state of this place, without provisions, without stores — and without Indian Goods (which last is a matter of the highest importance), it is necessary, I fully agree with the General. Less can be expected, (if anything at all) than if I had received reenforcements, which I judge absolutely necessary. More I have never asked from you. I am certain of being well supported by the officers, which gives me almost all the confidence I have in the approaching battle.[2]

Barclay had the weather in his favour on Thursday, September 9. He needed to use his long guns from Fort Malden against Perry without letting Perry close on him. If he were too close, Perry would be decidedly stronger, with three brigs and six schooners heavily armed with 490 men. Barclay had three brigs and three schooners and 310 seamen. But the wind changed. The British could not keep Perry off. The battle, which began just before noon on September 10 and raged for almost four hours, inflicted terrible damage. The noise of the cannon were said to be heard at least 256 kilometres away.

In the awful quiet after the fight the wrecked ships of both squadrons sagged together. Sixty-eight men were dead, 41 British and 27 Americans. Another 94 British and 96 Americans lay wounded. One-armed Captain Barclay had a shattered thigh and a shot lodged in the shoulder of his only arm. All his officers were either killed or wounded.

The dreadful news did not reach Niagara until September 16. Everyone there knew what it meant: Procter's army at Amherstburg, without provisions for the winter and with the guns of Fort Malden sacrificed on the *Detroit*, would

Commodore Oliver Hazard Perry

Perry, born in Rhode Island, joined the U.S. Navy as midshipman when he was 13. When war broke out he was commanding gunboats on the eastern seaboard, but he requested duty on the Great Lakes. He was sent first to Chauncey at Sackets Harbor. Chauncey decided Perry could serve better on Lake Erie.

In the Battle of Lake Erie, he refused to surrender his wrecked ship, U.S. Brig Lawrence, *and was rowed under fire to take command of the U.S. Brig* Niagara. *When the battle ended, Perry had captured two ships, two brigs, a schooner, and a sloop. His battle report contained a terse oft-quoted phrase: "We have met the enemy and they are ours."*

be forced to retreat. The whole upper country would fall. The state of apprehension at the beginning of October is reflected in Thomas Ridout's letter:

> We expect some serious movement every hour, as the enemy are in great force at Fort George. [The enemy fleet was standing by as American troops were loaded into bateaux and there was great

Lossing, 708.

As the British Shannon *raked the American* Chesapeake, *the wounded Captain James Lawrence was carried below saying, "Don't give up the ship!" The crew had no choice as the British took the ship, hoisted their flag, and towed the damaged* Chesapeake *into Halifax Harbour.*

Commodore Sir James Lucas Yeo

James was 11 when he joined the Royal Navy in 1793. In March 1813, he became commodore and commander-in-chief on the Canadian lakes.

He arrived in Kingston on May 14. Two weeks later, he had a small squadron ready for action. With his 23-gun Wolfe, his 20-gun Royal George, 14-gun Earl of Moira, two eight-gun schooners, and several gunboats, he outshone Chauncey's American fleet. His superiority kept the supply lines open as his ships carried goods as well as soldiers across from Kingston to Niagara. This advantage lasted until late July, when Chauncey set sail with his new 28-gun General Pike.

As winter came on, it was back to the drawing board and the race to hammer ships together faster than the carpenters across the lake. In the spring of 1814, Yeo set out with two new frigates while awaiting completion of his St. Lawrence, which would be the most powerful warship ever on the lakes.

Land commanders clamoured for Yeo to do something decisive, but with Barclay defeated on Lake Erie and Downie killed on Lake Champlain, Yeo knew he stood alone — if he lost Lake Ontario, he lost the war. So the game of cat-and-mouse continued.

Commodore Isaac Chauncey

Connecticut-born Isaac Chauncey joined the U.S. Navy in 1799 and became commander of Lakes Ontario and Erie in September 1812.

Until the arrival of Yeo, Chauncey's small fleet controlled Lake Ontario, enabling the attack on York and aiding Dearborn's attack on Fort George. When Chauncey returned to Sackets Harbor from Fort George, he found that Yeo had already attacked his naval yards.

Action in 1813 included an encounter 19 kilometres south of York, in which Yeo's damaged ships ran for Burlington Bay. Chauncey followed but declined to fight in a narrow bay owned by the enemy.

Chauncey and Yeo took turns blockading each other's harbours, depending on who had biggest guns at the time. When the St. Lawrence was finally launched its superior 112-gun power meant that Chauncey could not come out of Sackets Harbor.

fear that they would land above the British and attack.] We are driving all the cattle from this part of the district toward the head of the lake. The Chippawa and Short Hills country is stripped of cattle, and today they have been driving them from the vicinity of the camps. The wagons stand ready loaded with the baggage which moves in the rear. I am sure we shall march soon.[3]

Instead, it became evident that the American Army was heading east. Between three and four thousand Americans were moving toward Sackets Harbor, under General Wilkinson; their intention apparently an attack on Kingston. James FitzGibbon soon had orders to march his men to Forty Mile Creek. The 49th Regiment, the 104th, and a corps of *Voltigeurs* (Provincial Light Infantry from Lower Canada) were being sent to Kingston with all possible speed. On October 4, the men embarked in bateaux and crossed to York. From there they re-embarked on October 5 and reached Kingston on October 11. General de Rottenburg was also proceeding swiftly to Kingston.

Fitz was gone from Niagara before the next piece of bad news arrived from the west on October 8. Procter's retreating army had moved east along the river Thames, followed by the American General Harrison. At least there they could fight out of reach of American naval power. At the battle of Moravian-town (113 kilometres up the Thames River), Procter had made his stand on October 5.

Tecumseh was with Procter, although the two men had long ceased to understand each other. Tecumseh failed to see how defeat in a naval battle forced Procter's land force to retreat. For Tecumseh and his people there could be no retreat. In his speech to General Procter on September 18, he expressed the position of his Native nation with his usual terse eloquence:

Father, you have got the arms and ammunition which our great Father sent to his red children. If you have an idea of going away, give them to us, and you may go, and welcome for us. Our lives are in the hands of the Great Spirit. We are determined to defend our lands, and, if it be His will, we wish to leave our bones upon them.[4]

At the battle of Moraviantown, Tecumseh and his Natives fought long after the 41st Regiment had retreated. Tecumseh and his closest leaders never retreated — they all died fighting. The Battle of the Thames took place just one year after Isaac Brock died. In that year, Tecumseh must have often longed for Brock's brand of British leadership. That day, Tecumseh died as Brock had died, fighting a desperate fight.

Twenty-eight British officers and 606 men were killed or captured in the fight, 246 British managed to escape. They soon found each other in the woods and managed an orderly retreat to Burlington. Harrison and his American Army turned back to Detroit. Meanwhile, the sick and sorry army at Niagara had also marched to Burlington. On the 14th, Lieutenant-Colonel Glegg wrote:

We arrived here on the twelfth, after undergoing a very harassing march for our poor fellow, particularly the numerous sick, whose pallid countenances cut me to the quick. The elements were most unkind during our retreat but anything was pleasing after quitting that sink of disease on the Twelve Mile Creek, where an inactive residence had nearly annihilated as fine a body of men as were ever led against an enemy.[5]

Thomas Ridout wrote to his father from Burlington:

The times are so gloomy that I know not what to say. We shall soon retreat to Kingston. Every preparation is making ... We had a most dreadful time from the Crossroads [Homer]. Upwards of three hundred men were straggling upon the road and wagons

Don't Give Up the Ship

In a June 1st battle that took place just outside Boston Harbor, the HMS Shannon *defeated the U.S.* Chesapeake. *As the British* Shannon *raked the American* Chesapeake, *the wounded Captain James Lawrence was carried below, saying, "Don't give up the ship!"*

Lawrence died of his wounds but his words lived on. During the Battle of Lake Erie, Oliver Perry, whose flagship Lawrence *was named for the fallen captain, flew a banner with the motto, "Don't give up the ship," in white letters on a blue background.*

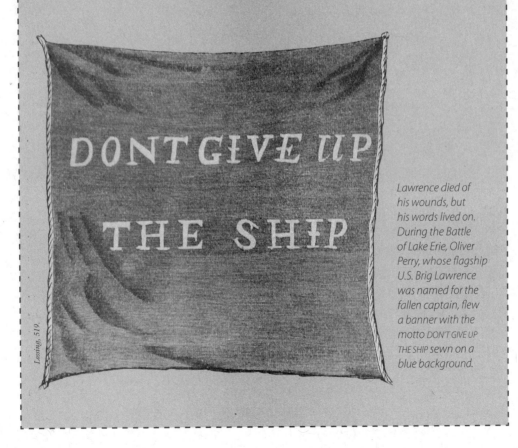

Lossing, 519.

Lawrence died of his wounds, but his words lived on. During the Battle of Lake Erie, Oliver Perry, whose flagship U.S. Brig Lawrence was named for the fallen captain, flew a banner with the motto DON'T GIVE UP THE SHIP sewn on a blue background.

loaded with miserable objects stuck fast in mud-holes, broken down and unable to ascend the hills, and the men too ill to stir hand or foot. One thousand Western Indians arrived last night from Detroit, besides 2,000 women and children. Poor creatures! What will become of them? It is said the great Tecumseh is killed.[6]

CHAPTER 11
RACING DOWN THE RIVER

The Governor-in-Chief and Commander of the Forces has the satisfaction to announce to the troops that the corps of observation, with the division of gunboats which he had ordered from Kingston to follow the movements of the enemy's army ... has completely defeated a large division of the enemy's army, consisting of cavalry, riflemen and infantry, exceeding four thousand men, which attacked it on the 11th November near Crysler's about twenty miles above Cornwall, taking from the enemy one field piece and four hundred prisoners.
— General Order, Headquarters, Lachine, November 13, 1813[1]

As FitzGibbon and his men pushed away from Forty Mile Creek, Fitz felt a new spirit take hold of him and his men. Not yet stricken by news of Procter's defeat and Tecumseh's death, they were ready to enjoy this journey east. Nearly all the men in the boats around him had had to deal with fever, many had hovered near death. Muscles were weak for the long pull on the oars to take them to York. But there was vigour in the air, a tang in the October breeze that you could taste, and a sky so solid a blue that you felt you could cut it with your sword.

These men of the 49th, 104th, and the *Voltigeurs* were embarking on a race and were keen at the starting line. Along the south shore of Lake Ontario, their Yankee competitors had a head start; they also had the advantage of deciding where the race would end. The British leaders could only guess that the destination would be Kingston. But some of the soldiers bet their boots that the Americans intended to attack Montreal. Nobody knew where or when the two racing fleets would meet, but they knew that some of the men in these boats would die when they did. In the meantime, each man would enjoy the race and be glad he had not died of fever at Niagara.

Their burst of energy long gone, they were weary when they pulled in to York, but a night inside barracks was a rare treat to men accustomed to tepees or barns. In the morning, well fed and rested, they started the long pull for Kingston.

Frost in the air meant the end of disease. Fitz took deep breaths, pure, clean, and cold. He could feel new strength in his arms. As he looked over his own Green Tigers he felt good about them too; they were all so active and tough by nature that they were regaining power in great style. In some of the other boats the men were not so well and would be hard put to pull themselves from York to Kingston.

Apart from the war, Fitz had another reason to be glad that he was moving east. He loved a girl named Mary Haley and it was a long time since he had seen her. She was the daughter of George Haley, a British soldier who fought under Burgoyne in the American Revolution, then settled on a grant of land in Leeds County.

War kept Mary and James apart but she was always there in the back of his mind. Sometimes it was hard for him to picture her face exactly but her presence was there, the warmth and joy, her importance to him. If he had a life to live after the war, he wanted to live it with Mary.

As it turned out, Fitz and the rest of the advance troops had almost a month in Kingston. Mary may have travelled there to see him. It is unlikely that he could go farther east to her home, as he and the rest of the 49th were part of a "corps of observation" that would be sent in pursuit whenever the Americans made a move out of Sackets Harbor.

If the British assumed the Americans knew where they were going, they were wrong. Back in August, John Armstrong, the Secretary of War, had spelled out the need to either attack and capture Kingston or go down the St. Lawrence and cut off communication above Cornwall (roughly where Morrisburg now stands). Major-General Wilkinson, who had command of the American Army from Lake Champlain to the Niagara frontier, had hurried up to Niagara but immediately got the fever. So there he stayed until October 2, when the British witnessed his departure with Chauncey's fleet and 6,000 troops.

On their voyage to Sackets Harbor the Americans got caught in severe storms. News carried to Kingston by a spy was that a number of boats had been driven on shore and half of their provisions lost. The spy also reported that Wilkinson had intended to attack Kingston, but on hearing that the British fleet had arrived there with reinforcements, had changed his mind.

On October 17, Wilkinson moved his troops to Grenadier Island, 29 kilometres from Kingston, poised either for an attack on that town or for a run down the St. Lawrence River. Meanwhile, he was writing to the Secretary of War and to Major-General Wade Hampton, in command of the Lake Champlain army, proposing an attack on Montreal and telling Hampton when and where to meet him. Wade Hampton happened to have an intense personal dislike for Wilkinson, and was not inclined to take orders from him.

Meanwhile, the hapless men of the American Army waited on Grenadier Island, victims of the indecision of their superiors and an overdose of rain, wind, and snow. As an officer wrote on October 26:

> Here we are at the east end of Lake Ontario, pelted daily with the inexhaustible rains, which seem to be collected and poured upon us from all lakes and swamps between this and Lake Superior. We have indeed for nearly a month been exposed to such torrents as you have no idea of in your part of the world. In consequence of the bad weather our troops from Fort George and Sackett's Harbor have been scattered everywhere along the coast, many having staved their boats, but most of them have now arrived here.[2]

On November 1, Wilkinson wrote, "The wind and waves and rains and snow still prevail, and we have made several fruitless attempts to turn Stony Point, one of them at great peril to three thousand men, whom I seasonably remanded to the harbour without the loss of a life."[3]

Snow was falling on Canadians as well, as Thomas Ridout could testify. While FitzGibbon and most of the troops moved east by water, Ridout and the Commissariat Department were travelling by land. They had left Burlington on the 18th and Thomas had a day at home in York before they pushed on. It took an incredible 10 days to get from York to Kingston. On November 1, he wrote of the miserable journey they had:

We have had a most harassing journey of ten days to this place, where we arrived last night in a snow-storm. It has been snowing all day, and is now half a foot deep. The journey has knocked Mr. Couche up. He is in the next room with a fever. Frequently I had to go middle deep in a mud-hole, unload the wagon, and carry heavy trunks fifty yards, sometimes waist-deep in mire, and reload the wagon. One night it upset going up a steep hill in the woods. Gee and I carried the load up to the top, whilst Mr. C. rode on three miles in the rain for a lanthorn. About eleven o'clock we got in, when we missed a trunk with 500 guineas in it. Mr. Couche and I immediately rode back about two miles and found it in a mudhole....

Accounts have just arrived from Montreal saying that four hundred of our troops have defeated General Hampton's army of four thousand men.[4]

The battle Ridout referred to would be known as the Battle of Châteauguay (October 25–26), and would become a proud piece of Canadian history. Armstrong had ordered Hampton to move 4,000 men from New York State up the

Châteauguay River to where it empties into the St. Lawrence, close to Montreal, and once there "hold the enemy in check," while awaiting Wilkinson.

On the Canadian front, Lieutenant-Colonel de Salaberry led his *Voltigeurs*, several militia companies, and some Natives a few miles up the Châteauguay where he prepared a defensive reception for the Americans. Hampton sent 1,500 Americans, under Colonel Purdy, on a circuitous 24-kilometre trail through the woods to outflank de Salaberry's men. They got thoroughly lost. In the morning, Hampton's main body attacked de Salaberry's advance picket of 300 militia and a few Natives on the left bank, while Purdy's detachment finally found and attacked the 160 militiamen on the other side of the river.

Behind de Salaberry, the Canadian rearguard was led by Lieutenant-Colonel "Red" George Macdonnell, whose 1,130 men sent up a tremendous racket in the woods to unnerve the Americans. Hampton began to withdraw his army up the Châteauguay and back over the border into New York State.

The Battle of Châteauguay was fought without the British Army. All the defenders were Canadian. Their successful rout of the Americans sent a wave of pride up the St. Lawrence and made young Canadians like Ridout eager to get on with the awful journey east.

FitzGibbon and the rest of the British also took new heart. They had embarked with the Lake Erie defeat ringing in their ears. Hard on their heels had followed the news of Procter's defeat in the west. This victory in the east was like a dose of good medicine that they all needed. If they were destined to meet the entire American Army at Montreal, it was good to know de Salaberry and his men would be there too.

It was becoming evident that they *would* meet at Montreal. By November 5, Wilkinson's entire army was on the move through the Thousand Islands: four regiments of infantry, two of Dragoons, and three of artillery. Chauncey had moved his fleet into the river to protect the troops. He would stay there until the army could pass below Prescott, then "use every exertion to get out of the river as soon as possible." On November 6, Wilkinson wrote to Hampton, "I am destined to and determined on the attack of Montreal if not prevented by some act of God, and to give security to the enterprise, the division under your command must co-operate with the corps under my immediate orders."[5] That same day, de Rottenburg released his "corps of observation" after the Americans.

FitzGibbon says they left about ten o'clock at night, under the command of Lieutenant-Colonel Joseph W. Morrison of the 89th. Fitz's own regiment was reduced by the previous campaigns to little more than 200 strong. The 89th amounted to 450 men. They had a few artillerymen and two 6-pounder field guns. They travelled in two schooners under the command of Captain Mulcaster (Yeo's favourite officer) along with seven gunboats and a number of bateaux. Mulcaster's armed schooners could go no farther than Prescott but his gunboats would take care of any Americans boats that lagged behind downriver.

Prescott — The Vulnerable Place

Surgeon "Tiger" Dunlop, an astute observer, declared the Americans could have cut the British supply line with a corps of riflemen and four field guns aimed at the Prescott shore. Later, historians would agree with him.

At the beginning of the war, Ogdensburg people were reluctant to fight their nearest neighbours and trading partners. In spite of Jefferson's 1807 trade embargo, trade remained brisk. Prescott people were still crossing the river under a white flag to trade potash and furs and shop in Ogdensburg stores. Even Jacob Brown, who would become an American general, was so heavily involved in trading potash with the enemy that he was nicknamed "Potash Brown."

Militia Captain Benjamin Forsyth was the American fly in this ointment of peace. In September 1812, he attacked Gananoque, wounding four men and taking eight prisoners. British leaders rushed to build blockhouses, construct Fort Wellington, and station a garrison there.

From Ogdensburg, under the command of Brigadier-General Jacob Brown, guns were firing on the British convoys. On September 16, they launched the Durham boat attack on FitzGibbon's flotilla near Toussaint Island. In February, Forsyth attacked

The St. Lawrence has never seen, before or since, such a sight as the movement of the American Army of 8,000 to 10,000 men down to Montreal. Three hundred bateaux swept along, as well as a variety of other small boats, followed by 11 gunboats to protect their rear. Thomas Ridout, as he travelled the Canadian shore, recorded the colour and commotion, the splendid pageantry, and the shock wave of alarm as they moved along. From Prescott he wrote:

> It was a grand sight to see an army of 10,000 men going down the Gallette rapids. They fired at us several shots, taking our wagon for artillery, I suppose. Every boat had a gun mounted, and carried about sixty men. About 180 immense boats went down full of men, besides schooners with provisions … The Americans seem

Elizabethtown (Brockville), released prisoners from the jail, and captured guns and ammunition. Lieutenant-Colonel "Red" George Macdonnell, temporarily in charge at Fort Wellington, decided to retaliate. He took 580 of his Glengarry Light Infantry out on the ice, pretending they were on their regular drill exercise, then attacked the Ogdensburg fort and barracks, driving the garrison out of the fort. Macdonnell took 70 prisoners, burnt the barracks, two schooners, and the gunboats, and carried off the military stores. For the rest of the war there was no garrison at Ogdensburg.

Why did the Americans not launch an all-out offensive in this vulnerable place to cut the British supply line?

Historian Alan Taylor believes a man named David Parish, an Ogdensburg multi-millionaire who had a tract of land along the river, used his influence with the government to keep the war away from his settlement.

On the Canadian side, Colonel Pearson at Fort Wellington understood the strategic importance of keeping peace across the river. He also understood the value of a little espionage whenever he and his officers were invited over to dine with the Americans. Often, they came away with some useful bits of news.

The narrow place in the river remained open for travel. The supply line was never cut. The British continued to move their army and its provisions up the St. Lawrence.

Lossing, 650.

Wilkinson's army moving through the Thousand Islands was a "grand" but alarming sight to those watching from the shore.

confident of taking Montreal. I never witnessed such a beautiful sight as the army going down the rapids.[6]

While Ridout stopped at Prescott, Morrison's corps of observation had arrived and collected a detachment of 240 troops commanded by Lieutenant-Colonel Pearson, consisting of two flank companies of the 49th, some Canadian Fencibles, three companies of *Voltigeurs*, and a few militia artillerymen with a 6-pounder gun as well as a few Dragoons to carry messages. Ridout wrote, "Yesterday Colonels Harvey and Pearson left us with 1,500 regulars and eight gunboats in pursuit, determined to attack the enemy wherever they are to be found."

Although Ridout guessed at 1,500, Morrison's force actually amounted to 900 men. They must have looked like a tiny fish determined to bite the tail of a whale.

On November 6, Wilkinson stopped 11 kilometres above Ogdensburg in order to "pass Prescott this night after the setting of the moon." He landed his men above Ogdensburg and sent each bateau down with a picked crew while gunboats guarded their front and left flanks against the guns of Fort Wellington. Most of the troops — and the powder and ammunition — were moved by land past the British batteries to re-embark below Ogdensburg. Downriver from Prescott, every farmer seemed to be on the shore taking shots at the Americans floating past.

A Canadian Paul Revere

Lieutenant Duncan Clark was 28, a member of the Incorporated Militia, and stationed at Prescott. On November 1, Lieutenant-Colonel Pearson sent Clark to Elliott Point, eight kilometres above Brockville, with precise instructions: "You will upon the appearance of an enemy, instantly take horse, and repair to Prescott, with all possible diligence, alarming the country as you pass down."

When Clark saw the American flotilla approaching, his order to "instantly take horse" gave him a problem because he had no horse. With no time to waste, he helped himself to the first farm horse he could find and set out as fast as the old horse could go, yelling out his news as he passed people on the road. At Prescott, he reported to Pearson that the Americans were approaching in 300 boats, bateaux, and gunboats.

His ride has been compared to that of Paul Revere. Revere had warned the Americans that the British were coming; Duncan Clark warned the British/Canadians that the Americans were coming.

When Wilkinson had had enough of this sport, he ordered 1,200 troops to land at Point Iroquois and drive them off. This formidable array of Americans nearly captured young Ridout. In his letter from Prescott he describes his close call:

> Good fortune attends me, for there never was a more narrow escape than when the Yankees landed twelve miles below Prescott. We slept within 200 yards of them. Mr. Green was taken prisoner three minutes after he had left us. Next morning they departed, and Mr. Couche sent me down to reconnoitre and inquire for him. I rode down two and a half miles, but the whole river above and below was covered with their boats; some pulled toward the shore where I was, and came within fifty yards, when a man came running to me and told me by all means to make my escape, for that six boats had landed above me. I instantly

Gord Mallory.

Fort Wellington at Prescott, started during the war to protect the river route, was finally completed in 1837.

galloped back, and passed before they reached the road, as they had landed on a small wooded point 300 yards away. The man told me afterwards that I had hardly got out of sight, when they took three prisoners.[7]

After this, Ridout and his party kept behind the "corps of observation," and Colonel Harvey, who was moving part of the corps east by land, "promised to clear the road."

Enid Mallory.

The monument to the Battle of Crysler's Farm was on land flooded by the Seaway project and has been moved to a hill beside Upper Canada Village, overlooking the St. Lawrence River.

From the 2nd of November until the 10th, the weather had been clear, dry, and mild. But on the night of November 10, cold sleet fell, showing no favour to either army. In the vicinity of present-day Morrisburg, British, Canadian, and American soldiers crawled under their boats or huddled beneath lean-to shelters or, if very lucky, found a friendly barn. Lieutenant-Colonel Morrison was snug and dry; he had established headquarters in John Crysler's big farmhouse. He liked the look of the terrain there as well as any for meeting the enemy.

Gord Mallory.

An immense mural of a battle scene, painted by A. Sherriff-Scott R.C.A., is displayed at the visitor centre below the monument.

The Americans had stopped just below Crysler's, at the head of the Long Sault Rapids. Wilkinson, unwell for most of this trip, suffered another acute attack of fever. He sent Brigadier-General Jacob Brown ashore with 2,500 men to clear the way to Cornwall. Meanwhile, Brigadier-General John Parker Boyd was to take the troops that could be spared from getting boats through the Long Sault Rapids, and turn back on the British force.

The rain had stopped by Thursday morning, November 11. The morning was bleak and cold and grey when Boyd's 2,000 regulars advanced on John Crysler's farm. The 49th and six companies of the 89th were positioned facing east along a road that ran north from the farmhouse, with log fences for cover. They looked toward a field of fall wheat and beyond it to where the King's Road crossed two gullies and a large ravine. Between the two gullies and stretching to the river,

Morrison had placed Pearson's detachment from Prescott. Three companies of the 89th, with three 6-pounder guns, protected Pearson's men on the inland side. Three companies of *Voltigeurs* were placed in the large ravine as skirmishers and about 30 Natives waited in the woods.

The Americans soon got past the grey-clad *Voltigeurs*, but at about two o'clock they were stopped by the 49th and 89th. FitzGibbon, in a letter written years later, said:

> The 49th wore their gray great-coats, while the 89th appeared in their scarlet uniform. General Covington, supposing the men in gray to be Canadian militia, called aloud to his men saying, "Come lads, let me see how you will deal with these militia men," but on their advancing the 49th, who as yet were calmly standing in open column under the fire of the enemy's skirmishers, quickly wheeled into line and commenced firing regularly by platoons which soon threw the advancing Americans into confusion and drove them back beyond the range of fire.

The British regiments were fighting on open ground, in formation, the way they were trained to fight. The Americans tried to get around the British on their left, but Morrison wheeled the 89th around to stop them. Captain Mulcaster's guns were attacking Wilkinson's headquarters boat. FitzGibbon finishes the story:

> General Covington being killed, the Americans soon after retreated to their own shore and ultimately went into winter quarters, abandoning altogether their intended attack upon Montreal.[8]

The final blow to Wilkinson was a letter received the next morning from Hampton, who refused to meet him at St. Regis. Wilkinson, tired and sick on that grey November morning on the St. Lawrence, was facing his own failure. There would be no attack on Montreal.

CHAPTER 12

DEVASTATION AT NIAGARA

From the St. Lawrence to the ocean an open disregard prevails for the laws prohibiting intercourse with the enemy. The road to St. Regis is covered with droves of cattle and the river with rafts destined for the enemy. The revenue officers see these things but acknowledge their inability to put a stop to such outrageous proceedings. On the eastern side of Lake Champlain the high roads are found insufficient for the supplies of cattle which are pouring into Canada. Like herds of buffaloes, they press through the forest making paths for themselves.
— Major-General Izard to the Secretary of War, camped near Plattsburg, July 31, 1814[1]

The end of 1813 was, for FitzGibbon, the end of his association with the 49th. Actually, by then there was little left of the 49th. From a regiment of 10 companies that Brock had proudly called one of the best in 1812, by the time of the Battle of Crysler Farm the 49th had been reduced to 160 men by the ravages of war. At that battle, Thomas Ridout says the 49th lost 60 more men, killed or wounded. Each of the 49th left alive to celebrate that Christmas of 1813 in Montreal must have considered his hold on life a kind of miracle.

Christmas in Montreal was a time of celebration for Fitz and all the redcoats who filled the streets. The disheartened Americans were camped in winter quarters on the Salmon River, south and east of Cornwall, while British soldiers danced in Montreal. After the privations and sufferings of the year past, it was almost unreal to attend a ball or sleep in a bed or eat Christmas goose.

Knowing what 1814 would bring, the soldiers enjoyed these brief good times even more. News from the Niagara frontier indicated that this would no longer be a "nice" war involving only professional soldiers and volunteer militiamen. When the Americans left the Niagara frontier to sweep down to Montreal, Brigadier-General George McClure had remained with a handful of troops to guard Fort George. When two new British commanders, Lieutenant-General Gordon Drummond and Major-General Phineas Riall, arrived in Upper Canada, McClure guessed that he was no longer safe in Fort George. On December 10, a cold, damp winter day, he decided to withdraw across the Niagara. Urged on by the Canadian traitor Joseph Willcocks, McClure burned the town of Newark (Niagara-on-the-Lake) after turning 450 women and children out into the snow. He gave them half an hour to carry away something for their survival.

When Drummond arrived with Colonel Murray of the 100th Regiment, the town was still smoking. The two leaders lost little time deciding to retaliate.

On December 19, Colonel Murray took the flank companies of the 41st and 100th, some militia, artillery, and the Grenadier company of the 1st Royals across the Niagara River. Soon a British flag flew over Fort Niagara. Murray was delighted to seize a large quantity of clothing, tents, and camp equipment, which would help the suffering townspeople at Newark.

A cannon fired from Fort Niagara was a signal of Murray's success to General Riall, who waited at Queenston. Riall's troops then crossed the river and destroyed Lewiston. It was to be a black Christmas for Americans living along the Niagara, caught in a relentless wave of British vengeance. A few nights later, troops again crossed over to burn Youngstown, Tuscarora Village, Fort Schlosser, Black Rock, and Buffalo. A letter from a gentleman at Canandaigua, published in the *National Advocate*, New York, December 31, portrays the full horror of the time.

Enid Mallory.

Canadians looking across the mouth of the Niagara found the American Fort Niagara too close for comfort.

The Indians and British are in the full tide of successful retaliation: 300 families (says Captain Parish, Indian agent) are now on their way to this place, and the most miserable sufferers, and many children without either stockings or shoes. All here is alarm and commotion, *O horrida bella! Horrida bella!* Porter's mills at Schlosser are burnt. Two sons of Benjamin Barton, Esq., are killed.[2]

In mid-January, Captain Fitz moved upriver to Kingston to join his new regiment, the Glengarry Light Infantry Fencibles. At the beginning of February, Wilkinson moved from Salmon River; 2,000 of his men went west to Sackets Harbor, under Brigadier-General Brown, and the remainder of his army withdrew to Plattsburgh.

As soon as the January thaw was over and the ice safe, the St. Lawrence came alive with the goings and comings of the army. During February, raiding parties crossed the frozen river to plunder sleighloads of provisions from Salmon River, Malone, and the Four Corners. Some of it was plunder that the Americans had taken from Canadian merchants the previous fall. By far the strangest activity on the river was the Americans bringing of sleighloads of flour and droves of cattle to supply the British Army. By then, Thomas Ridout was deputy assistant commissary-general, stationed at Cornwall:

> There are 1,600 troops there to be fed, and my duty will be hard, for the country is so excessively poor that our supplies are all drawn from the American side of the river. They drive droves of cattle from the interior under pretence of supplying the army at Salmon River, and are so allowed to pass the guards, and at night cross them over to our side. I shall also be under the necessity of getting most of my flour from their side.

On March 30, Wilkinson made a half-hearted attack on the British post at Lacolle River, then withdrew from military life. On May 1, 37-year-old Major-General George Izard took over the command at Plattsburgh.

Fort George

After Jay's Treaty (1796) gave Fort Niagara to the Americans, the British built Fort George on the Canadian side of the Niagara River opposite Fort Niagara. It was completed in 1802.

In May 1813, the Americans bombarded Fort George from Fort Niagara, firing red-hot cannonballs that set the wooden buildings on fire. As troops landed, General Vincent was forced to evacuate the fort and fall back toward Burlington Heights. When the Americans moved in they had to rebuild the fort they had burned.

The British recaptured Fort George in December 1813.

Parks Canada manages the fort today and offers tours of the officer's quarters, the barracks, blockhouses, the stone powder magazine, earthworks, and palisades. Enactors in the dress of the 41st Regiment talk about life in the fort and demonstrate musket loading and firing. As many as 1,800 Canadian and American scouts meet each year to re-enact the battle of 1813.

Guides at Fort George portray soldiers from the War of 1812.

Early in March, Quebec City cheered in the 2nd Battalion of the 8th Regiment and a detachment of the Royal Navy and Royal Marines who had travelled overland from New Brunswick. The men of the Royal Navy and Royal Marines were bound for Yeo's ships and continued on foot from Quebec to Kingston. When they reached that place at the end of March, they had been 53 days on the road.

Captain Fitz had a pleasant winter in Kingston, drilling his men to the high standards of fitness that he demanded. The Glengarries were an excellent regiment, as he knew from their record in battle. Previously, Fitz had worked with men who were Irish or British; these men were Canadian-born, mostly Catholic Scots from Glengarry County, east of Cornwall. His association with them would help to make him Canadian too.

Mary Haley was another influence making him Canadian. From Kingston he sometimes had time to travel east to Leeds County, where the Haleys lived, and spend a day with Mary and her family. Mary had knitted him enough socks to last out the coming campaign if he never stopped marching. She had heard too many stories of soldiers going barefoot on the Niagara Peninsula; she could not make shoes but at least she could supply socks.

When navigation opened on the lakes, Fitz had other things to think about. On April 14, he watched Yeo launch two new ships, the HMS *Prince Regent* and the HMS *Princess Charlotte*, which would give the British at least temporary superiority over Chauncey. The ships were ready to sail on May 3, and Yeo and Drummond decided on an immediate attack on Oswego, near Sackets Harbor, to capture guns, naval stores, and army provisions. Drummond had wanted to attack Sackets Harbor itself, but Prevost would not spare him enough troops from Lower Canada. He wrote to Drummond that the views of His Majesty's Government "do not justify my exposing too much on one shake. It is by wary measures and occasional daring enterprises with apparently disproportionate means, that the character of the war has been sustained, and from that policy I am not disposed to depart."[3]

Yeo had six companies of De Watteville's regiment, the light company of the Glengarry Infantry Fencibles, the 2nd Battalion of Royal Marines, and detachments of Royal Artillery, Royal Sappers and Miners, and Royal Marine Artillery.

They landed at Oswego in the morning, on May 6, and climbed a long, steep hill in the face of enemy fire, the Glengarries on the left flank. The Americans fell back from the fort and the attackers moved in to seize flour, pork, salt, seven long guns, and ordnance stores. The British loss was 18 killed and 73 wounded. But the guns for Chauncey's new ships, the USS *Superior*, and a brig under construction were not found. When it was learned that they were still at Oswego Falls, Yeo sailed off to blockade Oswego.

On the night of May 28, one of Chauncey's commanders attempted to get away with 19 bateaux carrying 21 long 32-pounder guns, 13 smaller guns, and 10 heavy cables. The British captured one bateau and found that 18 others were pulled into Sandy Creek, just 13 kilometres from Sackets Harbor, awaiting a further escort. One of Yeo's commanders, Stephen Popham, with three gunboats, four smaller craft, and 200 sailors and marines, went up Sandy Creek to attack them but had no idea that 130 American riflemen and 120 Oneida lay in ambush for them. The British were literally "caught up a creek." After losing 14 killed and 28 wounded, Popham surrendered his 200 men prisoners to the Americans.

The guns for the USS *Superior* reached Chauncey while Yeo, down-in-the-mouth, sailed back to Kingston. Chauncey's 62-gun ship would give the Americans command of Lake Ontario. Yeo would have to play mouse to Chauncey's cat until his own 112-gun ship, *St. Lawrence*, could be completed.

On April 14, Sir George Prevost, in Montreal, received good news from Lord Bathurst in London. A defeated Napoleon was banished to the Isle of Elba. Troops from Wellington's army would be available to fight in the Canadas. By June 3, he was writing that the 4th Battalion of the Royal Scots, the Nova Scotia Fencibles, and part of the 6th and 82nd Regiments were already on their way, amounting to 3,127 rank and file. Another 10,000 would be dispatched to the Canadas within the course of the year.

The Americans also got the news and knew how little time they had. After disagreeing all winter whether to attack Kingston in the spring (Armstrong had hoped Prevost would send troops to Lake Erie, thus weakening Kingston, which he could then take "by a coup de main"), it was decided in mid-March to fight again on the Niagara Peninsula. There, at least, they had an American-held Lake Erie behind them. With Fort Niagara in British hands they would use the Buffalo-Fort Erie entrance to Canada and then move on Fort George.

For the first time in the war, the Americans were bringing top-notch commanders and well-trained troops against the British. Major-General Brown, from Sackets Harbor, had come up from the New York Militia to be one of the best American generals. With him at Niagara was Brigadier-General Winfield Scott from Virginia, who was proving himself an able leader in the campaigns of this war. These two knew they had to act quickly.

Brown's army crossed the river above Niagara Falls early on July 3. Scott's troops crossed below Fort Erie, while another brigade under Brigadier-General Eleazer Ripley landed above. The two British companies that guarded Fort Erie soon surrendered.

When news of the attacks reached Fort George, Major-General Riall reinforced the garrison at Chippawa, six kilometres above the Falls. He was not aware, however, of the fall of Fort Erie, nor did he realize how superbly trained the Americans soldiers were until he took his 1,500 regulars, 300 militia, and Natives against Scott's advancing army on July 5. Although British and Americans were almost equal in numbers in the Battle of Chippawa, the British suffered severely, losing 148 dead compared to 48 Americans. Riall managed to get his troops back

Fort Niagara

A French fortification existed here as early as 1678 and was abandoned a decade later. Then, in 1726, the impressive stone structure known today as the French Castle was built.

An expanded Fort Niagara fell to the British in 1759 and remained British during the Revolutionary War. After the Jay Treaty was signed the fort was given to the Americans. During the War of 1812 the British captured it again in December 1813. At the end of the war, the Treaty of Ghent gave it back to the Americans again.

across the Chippawa, and two days later, when the Americans crossed upstream on the Chippawa, he fell back all the way to Fort George.

Captain Fitz and the Glengarries were waiting at York, until the 89th Regiment reached them. The 6th, 82nd, and 90th Regiments, sailing from Europe, were nearing Montreal but it would take considerable time to get them up to Niagara where the situation was desperate. Orders were quickly changed: "The Glengarry Light Infantry to be pushed on to Burlington without waiting for the arrival of the 89th Regiment, leaving all non-effectives at York."

Meanwhile, Riall had left sparse garrisons at Fort George, Fort Mississauga (built on Mississauga Point from the bricks and rubble of the burned town of Newark), and Fort Niagara, and had moved toward Burlington with close to 900 men. The 103rd Regiment, under Colonel Hercules Scott, was moving from Burlington to meet Riall at Twenty Mile Creek. Together they would attempt to attack the enemy's rear by the Short Hills and Lundy's Lane. The 103rd were at Twenty Mile Creek by July 15. Not far behind them was the Glengarry Regiment, marching from York.

Drummond wrote to Prevost from Kingston on July 13: "The enemy have established themselves at Queenston where they have placed guns on Mr. Hamilton's house and commenced fortifying the heights." Drummond travelled with the 89th Regiment and reached York on July 22 to assess the desperate situation. Getting men up to Niagara fast enough was one thing — finding provisions to feed them would be another. Two brigs loaded with provisions had reached York safely, and two brigades of bateaux were on their way, "which if they arrive in safety will further relieve us, tho' even then our supply will be very far from sufficient. I have therefore been under the necessity of ordering all the women and children, of the Troops, to be sent down from Niagara, Burlington, and York, and the families of the Natives to be placed on Half Allowance, with a view of decreasing as much as possible the issues." It was also becoming impracticable to keep the militia called out because this was harvest time and "the whole produce of the neighbouring country is in the greatest danger of being lost."[4]

While Drummond was worrying and hurrying to Niagara, General Jacob Brown, sitting with his American Army on Queenston Heights, was equally uncomfortable. Brown had counted on the cooperation of Chauncey's fleet to take Fort George but each day, as he looked in vain toward Lake Ontario, his exasperation increased. On July 13 he wrote to Chauncey:

> I have looked for your fleet with the greatest anxiety since the 10th. I do not doubt my ability to meet the enemy in the field, and to march in any direction over his country — your fleet carrying for me the necessary supplies. We can threaten Forts George and Niagara, and carry that place. For God's sake let me see you. Sir James will not fight; two of his vessels are now in the Niagara.
>
> If you conclude to meet me at the head of the lake and that immediately, have the goodness to bring the guns and troops that I have ordered from the harbour; at all events have the politeness to let me know what aid I am to expect from the fleet of Lake Ontario.[5]

His 2,600 troops, pressed close against Fort George, were in an extremely vulnerable position, unable to get supplies easily, with no reinforcements available, and harassed continually by the Canadians. Major McFarland of the 23rd U.S. Infantry wrote to his wife, "The whole population is against us; not a foraging party but is fired on, and not unfrequently returns with missing numbers." Finally, on July 19, the Americans burned every house between the Falls and Queenston, including the village of St. David's. McFarland wrote:

> This was done within three miles of our camp, and my battalion was sent to cover the retreat, as they had been sent to scour the country and it was presumed they might be pursued. My God, what a service! I never witnessed such a scene, and had not the commanding officer of the party, Lieut-Colonel Stone, been disgraced and sent out of the army, I would have resigned.[6]

Women in the War

Although little is heard of them, women were deeply involved in the War of 1812. On both sides of the border they cooked in the camps and the forts, did laundry, and nursed the sick and wounded. At Fort George, 6 percent of the soldiers were allowed to bring wives, who were granted half rations, their children a third of a ration. However, the women could often earn more than their husbands by doing laundry for the men. Unmarried women who were camp followers received no rations. When Native tribes joined the British camps, their wives and children came with them and received rations but sometimes were sent away when provisions were scarce.

A few women became war heroes. Laura Secord is well-known. On the American side, when Fort Niagara bombarded Fort George in 1813, a woman named Fanny Doyle was up on the mess-house roof "manning" the 6-pounder gun that fired red-hot cannon balls at Fort George.

Militia wives left alone to run the farm put in long hours of heavy work and often had to deal with marauding Americans or even hungry British soldiers stealing their hens and raiding their gardens. Some, like Mrs. Kirby and Mrs. Deffield, who helped save FitzGibbon in Lundy's Lane, actually fought off the enemy and some fought to save their homes from burning.

Gord Mallory.

When American cannon power burned the fort's wooden buildings in 1813 this stone magazine, built in 1796, was the only structure that survived.

By July 22, Riall had moved his forces up to Twelve Mile Creek. That day he sent Captain FitzGibbon forward with a party to reconnoitre and gain information of the enemy's intention. It was an old game to Fitz, played on familiar ground.

Fitz took his party up the heights of Queenston without being seen by an American. What he saw below him was the entire American army strung out in a column on the River Road, stretching from DePuisaye's House, near Newark, almost to Queenston. The wagons and baggage seemed to be halted at Brown's Point. The column began moving toward St. David's, and when about a thousand men joined the march in that direction it was again halted. From all appearances, the American army was falling back on Queenston. FitzGibbon had to leave the hill quite suddenly as a body of cavalry and riflemen advanced on him. He and his party escaped through St. David's, but were pursued by Americans for about a mile. As Fitz pounded through the heat of the July afternoon toward Twelve Mile Creek, he and his men were silent; the oppressive sight of that well-ordered blue army on Canadian soil set heavy in their heads. Each of them knew that hard fighting lay immediately ahead, the Americans desperate and determined to take this frontier before Wellington's troops could reach it.

Fitz was thinking that the summer of 1814 would be different from the days in 1813 when he and his Green Tigers had made the war a game and tailored it to their own talents. Grinning, Fitz remembered a day when he had doubled over with laughter inside a cave while the blue-coats above him were running in terror from his echo.

The grin faded. For the first time ever, James FitzGibbon was seriously considering the possibility of being killed. He wished he had married Mary Haley before he left Kingston. He was a captain now. If he died and Mary was his wife, she would receive the pension of a captain's widow. He could have left her at least that much. But how in the world could he marry her now?

He shook the thought of Mary out of his head and yelled at his men to ride harder. By three o'clock he had delivered his report of the American movement to Riall at Twelve Mile Creek. Riall, who had already written to Drummond once that day, hastened another letter off to him.

CHAPTER 13
THE BATTLE OF LUNDY'S LANE

On the evening of the 25th instant, at the Falls of Niagara, we met the enemy and had, I believe, one of the most desperately fought actions ever experienced in America.

— Colonel James Miller, Fort Erie, July 28, 1814[1]

The Battle of Lundy's Lane was fought within a mile of the Falls of Niagara. The roar of the great waterfall formed a background to the terrible noise and confusion of that horrendous scene. Today, the site is known as Drummond Hill Cemetery and in it Americans, Canadians, and British lie buried together.

The movement FitzGibbon observed on July 22 continued until Brown had reached Chippawa on the 24th. On Monday morning, July 25, Riall threw out the Glengarries and the Incorporated Militia (1,000 in all under Lieutenant-Colonel Pearson) as an advance guard to watch the enemy. They took up a position on a hill where Lundy's Lane crossed the Portage, or River, Road.

Lieutenant-General Drummond reached Fort George and took over command. On the Canadian side, he sent Colonel Morrison with the 89th to join Riall's 1,500 men already marching to join Pearson's advance at Lundy's Lane. On the American side of the river he ordered 500 soldiers and Natives under Lieutenant-Colonel Tucker to move out from Fort Niagara to attack Lewiston.

Gord Mallory.

The noise of Niagara Falls could be heard during the battle whenever the guns fell silent.

The enemy had moved out of Lewiston before Tucker could attack, so his troops crossed the river at Queenston to meet Morrison and Drummond on their way to Niagara Falls and Lundy's Lane. Part of the 500 joined Morrison's march; the rest were sent to defend Fort George.

When the Americans attacked around 6:00 p.m., Drummond had 600 men in line on the north slope of the hill, with two 24-pounder guns at the top. The

Gord Mallory.

In Drummond Hill Cemetery, Canadians, British, and Americans lie buried together, their lives lost in the Battle of Lundy's Lane.

Glengarry Regiment was positioned on the right. What followed was the fiercest, roughest, wildest fight in the war. British artillerymen were bayoneted in the act of loading their guns. Soon American guns were blasting within a few yards of British guns, while infantrymen were fighting hand to hand for control of guns and hill.

As darkness fell the confusion increased. Major-General Riall, badly wounded, was unfortunately carried by his stretcher-bearers smack into a party of American cavalry, who took him prisoner. On the hilltop it sometimes became impossible to tell which guns were whose; at one point, British soldiers loaded an American gun on their limber (front of a gun carriage) while the Americans limbered up a British gun, the two armies thus making a trade.

At about nine o'clock the firing stopped briefly. Brigadier-General Winfield Scott was down to 600 effective men, and Brown ordered the brigades of Ripley and Porter brought up to resume the fighting. The exhausted British began falling back until Colonel Hercules Scott's 103rd Regiment marched in from Burlington with 1,200 men. British and Americans fought in the darkness within paces of one another until almost midnight. Finally, with 171 Americans and 84 British killed, and more than 1,110 men wounded altogether, the firing ceased. With Brown and Scott both severely wounded, Ripley withdrew his exhausted and extremely thirsty men back to Chippawa.

An American doctor described the terrible scene on the hill the next day:

> The dead had not been removed during the night, and such a scene of carnage I never beheld, particularly at Lundy's Lane, red coats and blue and grey were promiscuously intermingled, in many places three deep, and around the hill where the enemy's artillery was carried by Colonel Miller, the carcasses of 60 and 70 horses disfigured the scene.[2]

The next morning saw the Americans throwing their heavy baggage into the rapids above Niagara Falls, destroying the Chippawa Bridge and falling back to Fort Erie.

General Drummond, suffering from a painful neck wound, was slow in following the Americans to Fort Erie. Had he moved faster he might have attacked a weak, unfinished fort, but the Americans worked day and night to build rear bastions and complete a deep ditch with two-metre earthworks and 800 metres of trenches and parapet breastworks along the shore. Near the shore a new stonework was built, which would be known as the Douglas battery, and on a sand mound called Snake Hill a new bastion, six metres high, would bristle with five guns.

THIS HALLOWED GROUND
REDEDICATED JULY 25, 1964
—— TO PEACE ——
WHICH HAS LONG ENDURED

CHEEKTOWAGA POST 2429
VETERANS OF FOREIGN WARS OF THE UNITED STATES

1814   1964

Gord Mallory.

This plaque erected by the Americans is an eloquent plea for peace between the two nations.

FitzGibbon had come through the Battle of Lundy's Lane unscathed. Drummond's report of the battle said, "The Glengarry Light Infantry, under Lieutenant-Colonel Battersby, displayed most valuable qualities as light troops." As Drummond moved forward, reaching the heights opposite Black Rock on August 2, he sent the Glengarries ahead driving in the American pickets. On August 4, he wrote of sending "a party of Dragoons and a few mounted men of the Glengarry Light Infantry by the road leading upon Fort Erie by Bird's and Tyce Horn's, along the lake shore, to make an accurate reconnaissance of the enemy's position."[3]

The British camp was set up in the woods about three kilometres from Fort Erie. British troops sweat to build a line of batteries about 550 metres from Fort Erie, from which to batter it down. While this went on, Fitz and his men were continually involved in skirmishes that recalled the Green Tiger days of the previous summer. American riflemen would attack their advance pickets and try to dislodge them or to spy out what the British intended to do next. Drummond wrote to Sir George Prevost:

> These attacks tho' feeble and invariably repulsed, yet harass our troops and occasion us some loss ... I cannot forbear of taking this occasion of expressing to Your Excellency my most marked approbation of the uniform exemplary good conduct of the Glengarry Light Infantry and Incorporated Militia, the former under command of Lieutenant-Colonel Battersby, and the latter under Major Kerby ... These two corps have constantly been in close contact with the enemy's outposts and riflemen during the severe service of the last fortnight; their steadiness and gallantry as well as their superiority as light troops have on every occasion been conspicuous.[4]

Dr. William Dunlop ("Tiger" Dunlop) was the army surgeon who dealt with the appalling number of wounded from the Battle of Lundy's lane. When these men had either died, recovered, or been sent to York, Dunlop became bored with his inactive life and transferred to the combat field before Fort Erie. Here he was in close contact with the Glengarries and their methods of bush warfare. He wrote of his admiration for their method of fighting:

> There a man ceases to be merely a part of a machine, or a point in a long line. Both his personal safety and his efficiency depend on his own knowledge and tact....
> Perhaps there can be no military scene more fit for the pencil than a body of light infantry awaiting an attack. The variety of

attitudes necessary to obtain cover — the breathless silence — the men attentive by eye and ear — every glance (furtively lowered) directed to the point — some kneeling, some lying down, and some standing straight behind a tree — the officer with his silver whistle in his hand, ready to give the signal to commence firing, and the bugle boy looking earnestly in his officer's face waiting for the next order....

The Glengarry Regiment, being provincials, possessed many excellent shots. They were not armed with the rifle, but with what I greatly prefer to that arm, the double sighted light infantry musket....

During the whole time we lay before Fort Erie, bush-skirmishing was an every day's occurrence, and though the numbers lost in each of these affairs may seem but trifling, yet the aggregate of men put *hors de combat* in a force so small as ours became very serious in the long run.[5]

Dunlop tells a story of getting lost with FitzGibbon:

One day, when relieved from picket, I announced to Col. P., who commanded our brigade, that I had discovered a short way through the woods to the camp, and accordingly I led the way, he and Captain F. of the Glengarries, following. By some fatality I mistook the path, and took a wrong turn, so that instead of finding the camp we came right on the top of an American picket, which opened fire upon us at about fifty yards distance. Being used to this we were behind trees in a moment, and the next were scampering in different directions at greater or less angles from the enemy.[6]

"Tiger" Dunlop's Army Medicine

The army medical department responsible for medical standards and hospitals was headquartered at Quebec City, far away from most of the action. Each regiment supposedly had its own surgeon and two assistants but scarcely a regiment had its full quota.

"Tiger" Dunlop, a surgeon in the 89th Regiment, arrived in Canada in the late fall of 1813 in time to care for the wounded after the Battle of Crysler's Farm. That done, he was moved upriver to Prescott and Gananoque, then to the Niagara frontier as the wounded from the Battle of Lundy's Lane were arriving at Twelve Mile Creek — wagon after wagon bringing badly wounded men, until he had 220 patients. They were housed in what he called "a ruinous fabric, built of logs." It was known as Butler's Barracks, built during the Revolutionary War by Butler's Rangers. Wind blew through the cracks, bad in winter but an advantage in sweltering summer heat. Men lay on straw on the floor or stacked on berths along the walls.

Dunlop had one assistant. For two days and two nights he never sat down. On the third day he fell asleep on his feet, one arm around the post of a berth. He was laid out on the straw with the patients and slept for five hours before going back to work.

When a patient was stabilized he went by ship to the hospital at York (housed in the church). When most of his patients got better, died, or went to York, Dunlop was sent to Chippawa to run a temporary shelter for the sick and wounded. As they arrived he gave them first aid overnight, then sent them to Niagara by wagon in the morning. During the assault on Fort Erie, Dunlop was with the army carrying wounded men from the field and treating their wounds.

In the midst of the siege of Fort Erie, on August 14, 1814, Fitz astounded his friends by going off to Adolphustown, near Kingston, to get married. It is even more remarkable that his superior officers let him go. Once the thought of death had seriously crossed his mind, he could not shake it, and he wanted to marry Mary Haley before he was killed. Many years later, his friend, the authoress Anna Jameson told this story:

F said, that if his request was granted, he would be again at head-quarters within three days; if refused, he would go without leave, "For," said he, "I was desperate, and the truth was, ma'am, there was a little girl that I loved, and I knew that if I could marry her before I was killed, and I a captain, she would have the pension of a captain's widow."[7]

The leave of absence was granted. How he got to Adolphustown, 354 kilometres from the Niagara frontier, and back within three days remains a mystery. His granddaughter says, "Landing at the Carrying Place, he rode sixty miles to the church door."

If he travelled by water, he defied Chauncey's fleet, which had finally sailed from Sackets Harbor and appeared off the Niagara River on August 5. Chauncey then sailed off to Kingston to interfere with the movement of troops to the frontier, but he left small warships to blockade Fort George. On August 14, Sir George Prevost complained, "The Naval Ascendancy possessed by the Enemy on Lake Ontario enables him to perform in two days what our Troops going from Kingston to reinforce the Right Division required from Sixteen to Twenty of severe marching to accomplish … the route from Kingston to the Niagara frontier exceeds Two Hundred and Fifty Miles."[8]

With enemy ships hovering before Fort George, it might still be possible for bateaux to get away and follow the shoreline to York and the Carrying Place, but it is hard to imagine FitzGibbon making such a trip to and fro in just three days.

Anna Jameson says, "FitzGibbon mounted his horse, rode a hundred and fifty miles in an exceedingly short time, married his little girl, and returned the day following to his duties, and to fight another battle, in which however he was not killed."

Actually, it is close to 320 kilometres from Fort Erie to the Carrying Place and another 48 kilometres to Adolphustown. If he did ride a horse there and back in three days he moved with the legendary speed of a pony express. At any rate, he got there. Mary got there by travelling 50 kilometres from Kingston with the

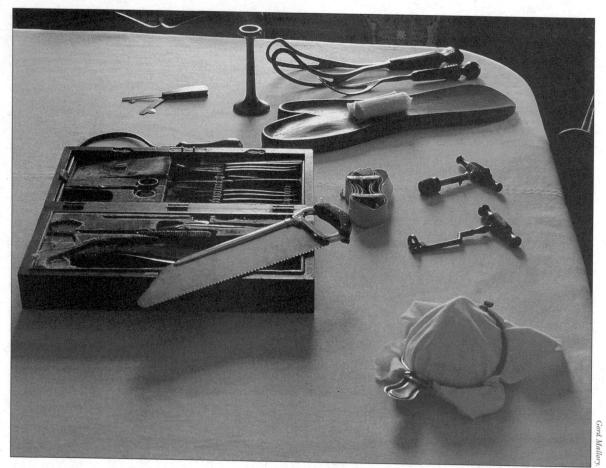

Gord Mallory.

An army surgeon's medical tools were simple; any available platform was his operating table.

Reverend George Okill Stuart, who married them. It is likely that Drummond took advantage of Fitz's flying trip to send dispatches that Mary and the Reverend Stuart would then carry on to Kingston.

Their marriage certificate, which is filed in the Synod Office of St. George's Cathedral in Kingston, states that:

John Le Couteur's Long March

Moving troops 1,200 kilometres into the interior of Canada could be as difficult as moving supplies. But there was an alternative: troops could walk. And walk they did. On snowshoes, pulling toboggans in the blizzards and sub-zero temperatures of February and March 1813, the 104th Foot marched from Fredericton, New Brunswick to Kingston.

At night, the weary men, who covered an average of 27 kilometres a day, built crude shelters from the cold. When they reached Quebec they had 10 days of rest, then walked to Kingston, arriving April 12. They had walked 1,100 kilometres in 52 days.

Most of the men left no record of their ordeal, but 18-year-old John Le Couteur did. He told of the suffering from frostbite, hands too cold to hold the salt pork over the fire, the fire that engulfed one hut and their struggle to put out the flames, the joy when they reached the St. Lawrence River and met a horse and cutter bringing provisions from Quebec, the excitement when they reached Kingston and saw the squadron of ships frozen into Lake Ontario.

John Le Couteur was sent to Niagara, where he was often employed running messages to the Americans. In the battle of Fort Erie, when the magazine blew up, John was thrown six metres into a ditch but discovered he was alive and unhurt. When he found out that Colonel Scott and Colonel Drummond (nephew of Sir Gordon) were both killed, he burst into tears.

James FitzGibbon, Captain in his
Majesty's Glengarry Lt. Infantry Fencibles
was married to Mary Haley (by licence)
by me George Okill Stuart
on the 14th day of August, 1814.

Mary Agnes FitzGibbon says her grandfather said goodbye to his bride on the church steps and rode back to keep his word to his colonel.

CHAPTER 14

THE BATTLE OF FORT ERIE

Captain FitzGibbon ... has this moment arrived at my headquarters with the full confirmation of this rumour. The enemy evacuated Fort Erie early this forenoon, having first blown up the works and in every other respect completely destroyed and dismantled the place, an event on which I offer Your Excellency my sincere congratulations. Captain FitzGibbon rode through every part of the place, in which the enemy had left nothing except ten or twelve kegs of damaged musket ball cartridges.
— Sir Gordon Drummond to Sir George Prevost, Falls of Niagara,
November 5, 1814[1]

FitzGibbon came back from his August wedding to a less-than-merry camp. Two days before, Drummond had launched his men in three columns against Fort Erie. One unit waded along the Lake Erie shore, aiming to get to the rear of the camp; they were entirely captured. Two columns, led by Colonels Drummond and Hercules Scott, fought desperately to gain the northeast bastion. At daybreak, powder stored in a magazine ignited and the northeast bastion exploded. The result was instant death for many of the British. Those who survived ran for their lives. Among those who died were Colonel William Drummond, nephew of General Drummond, and Colonel Hercules Scott of the 103rd.

Gord Mallory.

This painting of Fort Erie in 1804 by Edward Walsh, surgeon to the 49th Regiment, shows a favourite pastime of the soldiers — shooting passenger pigeons.

The army was in danger of starving. As long as Chauncey ruled the water, flour and pork could not be brought in to feed the troops. The road between Kingston and Niagara was so poor that it was not practical to send loaded wagons over it. On August 18, Drummond wrote of his army's needs: "Its wants in provisions, ammunition and stores of every kind, have become so alarmingly great and urgent that nothing but the assistance of the whole of H.M. squadron on Lake Ontario can enable it to continue its operation." Again, on August 21, he wrote of their need for ammunition, artillery, and artificers to build some sort of shelter for the men:

We possess no means of making anything like adequate preparations for covering the troops which it may be necessary to retain on this frontier during the approaching winter.

Stores of every description, particularly stoves, of which there are abundance at Kingston ... It is by the squadron *alone* that relief can reach us, and from the accounts I have lately received of the state of forwardness of the new ship, I really begin to fear that relief by this mode may not reach us in time.[2]

Two officers were sent through the countryside to induce each farmer to thresh his grain early and sell from five to 12 bushels to the army to enable it to hold out. Major-General Stovin, at Kingston, sent forward a large detachment of bateaux, laden with provisions and stores. Another stroke of good luck was the disappearance of the war vessels blockading Fort George. Drummond hurried the schooner *Vincent* off to York with the prisoners and the sick, and sent after it the schooner *Netley* and the brig *Charwell*. At York the schooners waited for the 97th Regiment, but before it arrived the two American ships returned. The 97th were reduced to walking to Niagara, and provisions could only be moved by bateaux.

In September, FitzGibbon was employed carrying dispatches to Kingston. He may have been sent post-haste to warn Stovin that the warships were back. Perhaps his superiors were kind enough to arrange for Fitz to have some time with his wife. His granddaughter says he travelled back to Niagara with Major-General Stovin on September 17. Drummond had requested that Stovin join him on the frontier as the neck wound Drummond had suffered in the Battle of Lundy's Lane was keeping him unwell.

News from the rest of the war brought alternate shock waves of hope and dismay. In midsummer, an American fleet of six vessels had attacked Michilimackinac but Lieutenant-Colonel McDougall, with 140 regulars plus militia and Natives, defended his post so well that they sailed away on August 5, the British flag still flying proudly over the northwest. Late in August, Canadians were almost as stunned as Americans to learn that a British force under Major-General Ross

> ### Peace Talks
>
> *Efforts toward peace were made throughout the war, but it was January 1814 before an agreement was reached to begin talks and talks did not get under way until August, in the city of Ghent. Demands that could not be met were made on both sides. Britain tried to support her Native allies by establishing a neutral buffer state between the United States and Canada, but the Americans flatly refused. United States wanted more Canadian territory and fishing rights off Newfoundland. Britain wanted part of Maine. Finally, both parties agreed to return to the status quo before the war, and signed the Treaty of Ghent on December 24, 1814.*
>
> *Before the treaty was formally ratified, the British attacked New Orleans on January 8, 1815, and were defeated. Peace was finally proclaimed on February 18 after both sides ratified the agreement.*

and Rear-Admiral Cockburn had moved up the Patuxent River on August 24 and burned the Capitol, the public buildings, and the presidential residence in Washington, D.C. Retaliation for the burning of York was complete.

While Washington burned, the peace talks that would eventually end the war were already underway at Ghent. The commissioners met there on August 8, and at first made little progress.

In early September, the British fleet and army moved up Chesapeake Bay toward the city of Baltimore. As they bombarded that well-fortified city, a young American lawyer wrote what would become the American national anthem.

The next news to reach Upper Canada was from Lake Champlain and was the worst the Canadians had heard for some time. On September 1, Sir George Prevost led an army of 10,000 into American territory with some of the best generals from Wellington's army. By September 6, they had reached Plattsburgh and awaited the British fleet on Lake Champlain under Captain Downie. British and Americans each had four ships but Downie's large ship, the HMS *Confiance*, was unfinished. Prevost rushed Downie into action before he was ready and, when

Lossing, 934.

After the British burned the president's residence in Washington in the summer of 1814, renovations and white paint made it henceforth "The White House."

cheering American spectators indicated British defeat on the water, Prevost withdrew his formidable army, which was already across the Saranac River and on the verge of taking Plattsburgh. Wellington's generals were furious; the stunned army fell back and returned in disgrace to Lower Canada.

Rain fell on the camp at Fort Erie for 13 consecutive days. Tiger Dunlop described the army's situation as "rather a bivouac than a camp, the troops sheltering themselves under some branches of trees that only collected the scattered drops of rain, and sent them down in a stream on the heads of the inhabitants, and as it rained incessantly for two months, neither clothes nor bedding could be kept dry."[3]

The army of 1814 was more healthy than it had been in the summer of 1813, but sickness began to appear in September. It was inevitable that it would spread as the men were camped in what amounted to a shallow lake. Drummond began to talk of falling back to higher ground on the Chippawa, but he was reluctant to stop work on the third battery. General Brown in Fort Erie could see that this newest battery "would rake obliquely the whole American encampment," and he determined to take it. FitzGibbon and Major-General Stovin returned from Kingston just before Brown's army attacked the British batteries on September 17.

At about three o'clock that afternoon, 1,600 Americans — militia and regulars — sprang out of the woods to attack the blockhouse at No. 3 Battery. Taking both blockhouse and battery from De Watteville's troops on guard, the Americans advanced to capture Battery No. 2. By the time they reached the third battery, the British regiments were out in force and a wild fight was underway.

The Glengarry Regiment was in the thick of it. In dispatches written later by Dr. Watteville, their part is described: "Lieut-Col. Pearson, with the Glengarry Light Infantry under Lieut.-Col. Battersby, pushed forward by the centre road and carried with great gallantry the new entrenchment, then in full possession of the enemy."[4] Under heavy fire, Brown was forced to pull back his troops. Later, Drummond wrote, "I myself witnessed the good order and spirit with which the Glengarry Light Infantry, under Lieut.-Col. Battersby pushed into the wood, and by their superior fire drove back the enemy's light troops."[5] By five o'clock it was over and the British line re-established as it had been, but 79 Americans and about 100 British had been killed and almost another 1,000 wounded.

Drummond decided the time had come to move back toward the Chippawa — the dreadful appearance of typhoid fever in camp hastened his decision. He described the condition of his men as extreme wretchedness: "Their present camp literally resembles a lake in the midst of a thick wood." At eight o'clock on the evening of September 21, they reached the site of their new camp and bivouacked for the night under torrents of rain.

In early October, General Izard marched 4,000 soldiers from Lake Champlain into Fort Erie, his total force was then 6,000 men. Drummond began to despair of his situation and lashed out in anger at Sir James Yeo for not daring to bring him the troops, newly arrived in the country but without transportation to the frontier. "I have, however, ceased to reckon upon any relief depending on the squadron ... Should any disaster happen to this division ... His Majesty's naval commander will in my opinion, have much to answer for."[6]

Meanwhile, Fitz and his Glengarries, posted in advance of the army, were busy at a pushing-back-and-forth type of warfare, as Americans advanced toward the

British camp at Chippawa and were repeatedly repulsed. Then, on October 18, more than 1,500 Americans were met by the Glengarries, the 82nd Regiment, and the 100th Regiment near the mills on Lyon's Creek. Afterward, Colonel Meyers, who led the British force, wrote:

> The conduct of the Glengarry Light Infantry during this campaign has been so conspicuous that Lieutenant-Colonel Battersby and the officers and men of that corps can receive little further from any report of mine, but on this occasion I cannot refrain from adding my humble tribute of praise to their well-earned fame.[7]

Brock's Monument

Ten years after the end of the war, a 41-metre monument to Isaac Brock was erected on Queenston Heights, near the place where he fell. Among the throngs of Canadians who arrived to honour Brock were numerous Americans.

FitzGibbon was there. He had helped to organize the procession and led the march as the bodies of Brock and Macdonell were moved 11 kilometres from Fort George to the monument, in a solemn three-hour march.

FitzGibbon's account said, "Of the thousands present not one had cause to feel so deeply as I, and I felt as if alone, although surrounded by the multitude. He had been more than a father to me in that regiment, which he ruled like a father, and I alone of his old friends in that regiment was present to embalm with a tear his last honored retreat."[8]

In 1840, an Irish Canadian ex-rebel decided to get at the Family Compact by blowing up Brock's monument. The damaged column stood until 1853, when the bodies of Brock and Macdonell were moved to a Queenston estate while the old monument was demolished and the new one built. In 1856, the bodies were moved again to be re-interred in the base of the structure. It soars 56 metres above the hill and stands 148 metres above the Niagara River, drawing thousands of visitors each summer.

Brock's Monument at Queenston.

Gord Mallory.

At last, on October 17, Yeo's fleet appeared at the mouth of the Niagara River. His new three-decked super-sized ship, the *St. Lawrence*, had finally sailed, bristling with 112 guns. Chauncey's fleet, as well as a small army under Brown, had already gone off to Sackets Harbor for fear of what Yeo and his big-gunned ship might do there. The arrival of the British fleet helped convince General Izard that maybe the game was up. The approach of a Canadian winter also helped to cool the ardour of the American attackers. In the afternoon of October 20, Izard started his army moving back toward Fort Erie. Finally, a report reached Drummond that the Americans were evacuating the fort, and he quickly sent Captain FitzGibbon with a small party of Glengarries to take a close look.

Fitz left his party in the woods and rode on alone. He stopped close to the fort and listened to the silence. The only sound that reached him was the wind rustling some leaves still clinging to the November trees. An eerie atmosphere hung over the site. Waving back to his men to stay put, he rode cautiously into the fort. The place was in ruins. They had destroyed, dismantled, or blown up all the works inside the fort. Nothing remained but 10 or 11 kegs of damaged musket ball and cartridge.

Sitting on his horse in the midst of the empty chaos, he experienced a great wave of elation that spread a wide grin over his face. This moment would always stick in his mind as the end of the war, although peace would not be official until March. Fort Erie was empty. Not one American remained on this side of the Niagara. He thought about Mary and the future he had not dared to plan. Maybe he had survived this crazy war after all.

He rode back outside the fort, let out a wild Irish yell, and motioned his men to come on in.

CHAPTER 15

AFTER THE WAR

I have resided in Canada, and in every city in it, east and west, for more than forty-five years, and few men have had such good opportunities of knowing its people as I have had; and few can feel a more ardent wish for their prosperity and happiness than I do; and I look to the future for all the British Provinces with the most cheering and confiding hope.
— James FitzGibbon[1]

Fitz tackled civilian life much as he would another battle; his enemies were the times he lived in, the political system, and, above all, his friends in the Family Compact whose entrenched positions made it difficult for men like himself to get ahead. It was inevitable that his allegiance should be with the Compact, men who had fought in the War of 1812 and imbibed a lifelong hatred of American democracy. Allied against the Compact were later immigrants from the United States, who brought American democratic ideas with them and clamoured for reform.

The allegiance to king and country of the sheriffs, magistrates, militia officers, and customs collectors who formed the outer circles of the Compact was equally strong, but their rewards were certainly less than those of the ruling elite. It was in this group that FitzGibbon found himself. He held a variety of jobs, all poorly paid. By 1827, he was clerk of the House of Assembly and colonel of the West York Militia.

James had first gone into debt when appointed to the adjutancy of the 49th in 1806, in order to buy his horse and uniform, and he remained in debt almost to his dying day. According to old friends, he was generous to a fault and many times went deeper in debt to help a friend. He also lived beyond his means in a two-storey house on 18 acres of land at Queen Street and Spadina Avenue in Toronto, with graceful willow trees, a bowling green, and spacious gardens filled with fruit and flowers.

The Family Compact

Sons of Loyalists who survived the war went on to fame and fortune as the rulers of Upper Canada. John Strachan, who defied General Dearborn when York fell to the Americans, was archdeacon of York by 1834 and the central star of the Family Compact. John Beverly Robinson, one of the eager young men who went with Brock to Detroit, became attorney general after Macdonell fell with Brock. By 1834, he was chief justice of Upper Canada, "the second most influential man in the province."

Christopher Hagerman, aide-de-camp to Sir George Prevost, became solicitor general in 1834. Archibald McLean was named chief justice of the Court of Queen's Bench. Alexander Hamilton, a militia captain, became sheriff of Queenston and member of the Legislative Council. William Allan, an officer in the war, became a wealthy merchant, president of the Bank of Upper Canada, and member of both the Legislative and Executive Councils.

Other familiar names find places in the outer circles of the Family Compact along with FitzGibbon. William Jarvis became sheriff of the Home District. William Hamilton Merritt, Fitz's hard-riding comrade of the Green Tiger days, became a political leader and promoter of the Welland Canal. Dr. "Tiger" Dunlop made financial hay with the Canada Company, which owned large tracts of land near Goderich. Thomas Ridout, the young man who stole onions and fence rails, helped to organize the Bank of Canada.

Anna Jameson, who came from England in 1833 with her attorney general husband, described the leaders of Upper Canada as "a stiff-necked gentry who have formed a petty kingdom in a raw lake port." Her husband was nominally one of them, but this did not prevent Anna from seeing things the way they were.

His first years with Mary were happy. They had happy, healthy children; a daughter Mary, then Charles, William, George, and James, then 12 more, none of whom survived. By the 1830s, Fitz spoke of his wife as delicate and unwell. When one considers that Mary was continually bearing and burying children, one wonders how she could remain sane, let alone well.

Fitz was known as a superb teller of stories, and a man who would do anything for a friend or a cause he believed in. Many of his friends were fellow Masons and for a number of years he was Provincial Grand Master of the Order.

According to his granddaughter, he had a habit of "interfering in whatever occurred within his cognizance whenever there appeared the remotest chance of such interference being for good, whether it was any of his business of not."[2] It was inevitable that he would make enemies too. By 1834, he had one particular enemy. William Lyon Mackenzie, who published a radical newspaper, *The Colonial Advocate*, ranted and railed against everything Fitz believed in.

Although politically on opposite sides, the two men were oddly alike. Both had been born poor and had educated themselves with fanatic determination. Both had an enormous capacity for work. Mackenzie often worked all through the night, pouring into printer's ink all the anger and frustration he felt toward the Family Compact. Of FitzGibbon, Anna Jameson says, "With so much overflowing benevolence and fearless energy of character, and all the eccentricity, and sensibility, and poetry, and headlong courage of his country, you cannot wonder that this brave and worthy man interests me; unluckily, I can see him seldom, his life being one of almost unremitting toil."[3]

Both were gifted orators. Fitz used his gift to entertain or, on several occasions, to restore peace and order. In 1823, he was sent by the Governor to Perth where riots had broken out between Protestant and Catholic Irish. His gift of speech was even more eloquent in Gaelic and he soon had a mob of angry men quieted as they listened to him. In 1826, he was sent to Peterborough where similar trouble threatened, and again the magic of his Irish oratory saved the day.

Mackenzie, on the other hand, used his colourful command of words to arouse and incite people against the government. He described the Family Compact as "official fungi, more numerous and pestilential than the marshes and quagmires that encircle Toronto." Settlers who had grievances against the government could not ignore this little Scotsman, who bent over their ploughshares and poured out volumes of abuse against the Strachans and Robinsons and Hagermans.

Both men led charmed lives and seemed impervious to personal danger. When cholera struck York in 1832, and again in 1834, both Mackenzie and FitzGibbon could be seen removing the sick to the hospital by cart and driving cartloads of dead to be buried.

In 1834, as the town of York became the city of Toronto, William Lyon Mackenzie was elected mayor to the disgust of staunch old Family Compact types. On July 30, a noisy public meeting was held in the marketplace. What happened there was an accident but it would stamp the image of Mackenzie on FitzGibbon's life in colours of horror and grief.

A lot of boys, including Fitz's sons, managed to find standing room on a balcony over some butchers' stalls. When Sheriff Jarvis spoke in support of a vote of censure against Mackenzie the crowd stamped and cheered, and the balcony collapsed. Several boys suffered broken bones but far more dreadful was the fate of the few impaled upon the great hooks of the butchers' stalls beneath. FitzGibbon's third son, George, was one of those unfortunates. Fitz, stunned with grief, carried the boy home to his horrified mother.

George only lived a few hours but in such pain that James and Mary could only be glad to see him go. The scar left on their lives never healed. His mother's physical health steadily deteriorated while Fitz seemed to bear the abrasion mentally. He worked ever harder, driving himself for king and country; he worried incessantly about the forces of democracy undermining the political system he believed in. In some deep recess of his mind he linked Mackenzie with the terrible death of his son. As the threat of rebellion increased, that red-wigged agitator became for Fitz a personal obsession.

The November 24 issue of Mackenzie's newspaper published what was, in fact, a constitution for the new state of Upper Canada. Throughout the countryside, Mackenzie had a network of vigilance committees that could serve as a military set-up in time of war. By December 1837, the writing was on the wall, but it was the bad luck of Upper Canada to have a new lieutenant-governor who couldn't read it. Sir Francis Bond Head was a blue-eyed, curly haired, rather handsome and winsome man, but curiously lacking in common sense. When Sir John Colborne had written to ask Sir Francis whether he could spare any troops for Lower Canada, where Louis-Joseph Papineau was leading a *patriote* revolt, Sir Francis replied that he would gladly send them all. When the last detachment moved from Penetanguishene through Toronto en route to the city of Quebec, Fitz begged Head to keep them. Sir Francis's lofty reply was, "I do not apprehend a rebellion in Upper Canada."

In 1834, FitzGibbon had formed a corps of young Toronto men that he drilled twice a week during the summer months. His granddaughter says, "Perhaps the happiest hours of these years were spent in this labour of love. He was a soldier before everything. He loved the very rattle of accoutrements." Now in 1837, those 70 young men, drilled by an old pro, might have to defend a city left without a soldier.

Six thousand stand of small arms and ammunition had recently been sent up from Kingston and were placed by Francis Bond Head in the market hall, where he had only two constables guarding them. Fitz offered to use his corps of young volunteers to guard these arms. Head, of course, refused.

By this time, Fitz was near distraction. He sat down and wrote a list of names, 126 men in all, whom he knew to be loyal citizens. He warned each of the men on this list to be prepared to come armed to the Parliament Buildings at any hour of the day or night when they heard the college bell ring an alarm. He also arranged that the cathedral bells be rung. Sir Francis was stunned, but Fitz did not stop talking long enough to let him say anything. Sir Francis, overwhelmed by the passion of FitzGibbon, consented. Fitz scurried off before the governor could change his mind.

On the 2nd of December, a Saturday, a fellow Mason reported to FitzGibbon that pikes were being forged at Lount's blacksmith shop at Holland Landing, and men were drilling every day in North York. Fitz hurried to Sir Francis with the news. Head and his council complained that the information was third- or fourth-hand. Fitz had at least one supporter, the Honourable William Allan, who rose and said,

"What would you have, gentlemen? Do you expect the rebels will come and give you information at first-hand?" Laughter broke the tension briefly. Allan finished his speech: "I agree in every word spoken here today by Colonel FitzGibbon, and think that an hour should not be lost without preparing ourselves for defence."[4]

Nothing was done until Monday morning, when FitzGibbon was summoned by Sir Francis and handed a militia general order appointing him adjutant-general of militia. As that post was already filled by Colonel Coffin, Fitz consented to be "acting adjutant-general."

On Monday night, FitzGibbon and friends kept an all-night vigil at his office in the Parliament Buildings, reporting events to Bond Head, who kept going back to bed. Fitz obtained definite information that the rebels had assembled 11 kilometres north on Yonge Street to march on the city. Three loyal Tories from Richmond Hill decided to risk riding through their pickets. Colonel Moodie was shot dead, Captain Hugh Stewart was captured, but the third man, named Brooke, got through and brought the news to the city.

The Moodie-Strickland-Trail Connection

FitzGibbon became acquainted with Susanna (Strickland) and her husband, Dunbar Moodie, when Fitz lived with his son William, in Belleville. In 1850, Fitz's son Charles married the Moodie's daughter Agnes. Agnes was an artist who would work with her aunt, Catharine Parr (Strickland) Traill, to produce the beautiful Canadian Wild Flowers *in 1868, and* Studies of Plant Life in Canada, *1885.*

Mary Agnes FitzGibbon was the daughter of Charles and Agnes. She would write the first biography of her grandfather, A Veteran of 1812, the Life of James FitzGibbon.

While living in England, Fitz got to know the four Strickland sisters who had remained in England. While Sara was not a writer, Elizabeth, Agnes, and Jane were all literary celebrities. Agnes was famous for her Lives of the Queens of England *series. Elizabeth had a cottage at Bayswater, where Charles often visited, and letters suggest that he and the sisters became close friends.*

Fitz had no time for Head now. One of his rifle corps was sent post-haste to ring the college bells. Fitz jumped on a horse and galloped through the west end of Toronto, shouting out to the men to assemble at the Parliament Buildings. Then he rode to the church, because the bells were not yet ringing.

Next he went back to City Hall, giving directions that the arms be distributed to the men as they arrived. He and two students then rode up Yonge Street as far as Rosedale (the estate of Sheriff Jarvis) and saw no sign of rebels. Fitz decided to turn back and arranged for a picket to be posted there. The boys, one a son of Major Brock of the 49th Regiment, wanted to ride on to reconnoitre Montgomery's Tavern. FitzGibbon let them go, but he was nervous for their safety. Suddenly, out of the night rode John Powell and a Mr. McDonald, also rebel hunting. FitzGibbon urged them to overtake the two boys.

When Fitz got back into Toronto he went to Government House. Head was actually up and Fitz was amazed to find him talking to John Powell, red in the face and out of breath, with a remarkable story to tell. Before he and McDonald could reach the boys, the two had been taken prisoners by Mackenzie, a Captain Anderson, and three other rebels. Powell and McDonald soon ran into the party and became prisoners too.

Mackenzie had left Anderson and Sheppard to take their prisoners to Montgomery's Tavern while he rode toward Toronto. But, nearing Montgomery's, Powell, who was forced to ride in front, suddenly delved for a pistol hidden in his coat, wheeled his horse, and shot Anderson in the neck. Anderson fell dead from his horse and Powell rode pell-mell for Toronto. Afraid he was being pursued, the portly Powell abandoned his horse at Davenport Road and ran, puffing, across Queen's Park and down College (now University) Avenue to Government House, where he had great trouble getting Mrs. Dalrymple to awaken her brother. But by the time Fitz arrived, Sir Francis was convinced — in fact, was close to panic.

It was a wild night in Toronto. Judge Jones had formed a picket and marched it out Yonge Street to the tollgate. At City Hall, Fitz had a mob from which to make an army, and he had no way to know who was friend or foe. Many of these men clamouring for arms might join Mackenzie with their weapons. But by Tuesday morning, the men were formed in platoons in the market square. A 6-pounder gun stood loaded in front of City Hall and men were working to barricade the windows of City Hall, the Bank of Upper Canada, the Parliament Buildings, Osgoode Hall, and Government House, with two-inch planks loop-holed for musketry.

While Fitz was forming a Yonge Street picket for Tuesday night, Bond Head forbade him from sending a man out, and gave FitzGibbon a positive order not to leave the building. Seizing Fitz by the arm with both hands, the governor exclaimed, "If you go through the city as you have heretofore done, you will be taken prisoner! If we lose you, what shall we do?"[5]

FitzGibbon ignored him, took Sheriff Jarvis with a picket up Yonge Street, then came back and told Head what he had done. That night, the picket stopped a motley force of rebels who had been sent toward the city for the purpose of setting it on fire.

When it was almost midnight, Sir Francis suddenly decided they should remove the spare arms to the Parliament Buildings, which were farther away and less liable to be burned. Fitz was horrified. In the darkness of night, the governor wanted each man to lay down his loaded weapon and march with a half-dozen unloaded arms to the Parliament Buildings. If a spy informed Mackenzie what was going on, the situation could quickly get out of control. The night was saved by the arrival of Allan MacNab, speaker of the House of Assembly, with 60 men from Hamilton. MacNab's men could guard all approaches and the arms would be safe where they were until morning.

By noon on December 7, 1837, Fitz had his grand army ready to march. There were 920 men. The main body, 600 strong, was led up Yonge Street by FitzGibbon, MacNab, and Sir Francis. A left wing of 200 men moved up College Avenue and on to the north, using side roads. A right wing, led by Colonel Jarvis, marched along east of Yonge Street. It was a fine bright day, and two bands raised the spirits of the soldiers. Many townspeople joined the parade and marched out to the scene of battle.

Jefferys, Vol. 3, 18.

These rebels marching down Yonge Street were intent on burning the Parliament Building.

That battle was one of the shortest in history. The rebel force that met FitzGibbon's 920 men was somewhere between 400 and 600 men. Only one man, Ludwig Wideman, was killed in the fray, although 11 Patriots were wounded and at least four died later. Fitz's army suffered five wounded.

Within minutes the rebels were fleeing in all directions. The one FitzGibbon desired most to catch had abandoned his horse and disappeared into the woods. (In the December cold with the entire Tory countryside hunting him, Mackenzie would manage to hide and slide his way to Niagara and cross into the United States.)

When FitzGibbon turned back to Montgomery's he found the tavern in flames. He had already met a party of 40 men heading north with orders to burn the house of David Gibson, one of Mackenzie's supporters. Not believing the order, he hurried ahead to catch Sir Francis. The governor's words to Fitz were, "Stop, hear me — let Gibson's house be burned forthwith, and let the militia be kept here until it be burned." Then the governor galloped away, leaving Fitz with the burden of the cruel order.

FitzGibbon's granddaughter says that had the order been given him in private, he would not have obeyed. But his military training made it imperative that an order given by his commander-in-chief in front of his men be obeyed. Fitz first ordered his field officer to carry out the governor's command, but the man implored him, "For God's sake, Colonel FitzGibbon, do not send me to carry out this order."

"If you are not willing to obey orders, you had better go home and retire from the militia."

"I am very willing to obey orders, but if I burn that house, I shall be shot from behind one of these fences, for I have to come over this road almost every day in the week."[6]

Fitz let the man go and took the party himself to burn the house.

This should have been FitzGibbon's finest hour. He had just saved the city of Toronto. But thanks to the machinations of Sir Francis Bond Head he had come to his lowest performance. David Gibson would be fleeing to the States so that he would not end up in jail facing a death sentence. Mrs. Gibson and four young children would be alone to face the Canadian winter. And there he stood burning their house.

By the time Fitz reached his own house that night, he was so exhausted that his children had to help him dismount. His mental state was even worse. The sleepless days and nights, the anxiety and frustration of dealing with Head, and the final meanness of having to burn Dave Gibson's house, had left him sick in body, mind, and soul. Nor was there any comfort in his home. Mary was sick. His youngest child was dying. Fitz himself was unable to get out of bed, but he sent a message to Sir Francis resigning his appointment as adjutant-general.

Farewell to Francis Bond Head

At the Mansion House Hotel in Watertown, New York, a strange little drama took place in March 1838. Patriot refugees, including Mackenzie, were staying there. But so was Sir Francis Bond Head. Convinced that he might be murdered en route, Head had left Canada furtively, like a criminal. He had travelled with Judge Jones, who posed as a gentleman from Kingston; Head was his valet. He and Jones had crossed at Kingston, paddling a small boat from one ice floe to another.

Head was recognized at the Mansion House, but treated with great courtesy by the rebel leaders, and left the hotel in a coach and four with the Patriots cheering him on his way.

In January 1838, the House of Assembly passed a resolution to reward Fitz for saving the city and possibly also the province, with a grant of 5,000 acres of Crown land. He got nothing until 1845 and then received £1,000 instead of land. It was September 1847 before any money was actually paid. He used it to pay off debt, but it had come too late to save his health. Financial anxiety, coupled with worry over Mary's health, had worn away at the old Green Tiger spirit. Mary had died on March 22, 1841, and was buried in St. James Churchyard.

After Mary's death, Fitz followed the government to Kingston. The Union Act of 1840 had created a single Province of Canada, uniting Upper and Lower Canada. Later, when the government was to move to Montreal, FitzGibbon was unable to go. He handed in his resignation in May 1846 with a certificate and letter from Dr. Widmer. The letter drew a tragic picture of the one-time hero of Beaver Dams, now a victim of the times he lived in, caught between the tides of reaction and reform. Widmer explained that his expectation of "release from pecuniary embarrassments …" and the frustrations that followed "had a powerful effect in destroying the healthy tone of his mind, and has rendered him incapable of performing the active duties of his office, and almost unfitted him for the social intercourse of his friends and acquaintances."[7]

But there was fight left in the old Green Tiger yet. His son, William, was clerk of the County of Hastings and his residence in Belleville became home to Fitz while he recovered. If his mind was in poor, confused state, he took care that his body be kept in good condition. Mary Agnes FitzGibbon wrote:

> The spectacle of a man turned of sixty-five years of age, clad in jerseys swinging himself from a bar fixed across the supports of the verandah, doubling himself up into a ball, jumping through his hands, or hanging by his feet, drawing his body up by sheer strength of muscle, and anon leaping over chairs arranged in rows, was quite sufficient to obtain him a certificate of insanity from the majority of his neighbours.[8]

By the beginning of 1847, FitzGibbon felt well enough to go to England. He received his pension, his mental health improved, and he never returned to Canada. He found old friends and made new friends, among them the sisters of Susanna Moodie and Catharine Parr Traill.

In 1850, FitzGibbon was appointed one of the Military Knights of Windsor, an order founded in the 14th century for the support of 24 soldiers "who had distinguished themselves in the wars, and had afterward been reduced to straits." He lived within the walls of Windsor Castle, opposite St. George's Chapel, received a small salary, and was required to attend services at St. George's.

There, his final years were passed sharing with the other knights a lively interest in worldly affairs both present and past. In the first year he starved himself to pay off debts, determined to die owing no man. His debt made it impossible for him to return to Canada, although he wrote to one of the young militiamen he had trained in 1837 of his longing for Canada. "Its future seems to me more full of promise than that of any other section of the human family. I long to be among you."

By far the happiest days were when a friend from the far distant past came to visit him. Fitz's association with the family of Sir Isaac Brock lasted all his life. The hero worship he felt for Brock stayed with him always. In a letter written late in life he refers to the Battle of Beaver Dams:

FitzGibbon, A Veteran of 1812.

James FitzGibbon, seen here wearing his Military Knight of Windsor uniform.

When I brought in those five hundred prisoners and delivered them up to General Vincent, I then thought I would have given the world's wealth to have General Brock there alive to say to him, "Here, sir, is the first installment of my debt of gratitude to you for all you have done for me. In words I have never thanked you, because words could never express my gratitude for such generous protection as you have hitherto unceasingly extended to me."[9]

James died on December 10, 1863. He was 83 years old. His children, William, Mary, and James had died in the 1850s; only Charles survived him.

In his last year, when almost unable to leave his bed, he questioned his doctor about the possibility of an ocean voyage home. There he could lie by his wife Mary, in the churchyard of St. James in Toronto. Instead, he was to die in London and lie in the catacombs of St. George's Cathedral, a long way from Niagara where the Green Tiger had fought so well in the war, a long way from Toronto where the public servant had fought the longer, devastating battles of the peace.

NOTES

Introduction

1. James Croil, *Dundas or a Sketch of Canadian History* (Montreal: Dawson, 1861).

Chapter 1

1. Anna Jameson, *Winter Studies and Summer Rambles in Canada, 1838* (London: Saunders and Otley, 1838), 57–58.
2. Mary Agnes FitzGibbon, *A Veteran of 1812: The Life of James FitzGibbon* (Toronto: William Briggs, 1898), 19.
3. *Ibid.*, 57.
4. James FitzGibbon to F.B. Tupper, September 12, 1846, F.B. Tupper Papers (Ontario Archives).

Chapter 2

1. E.A. Cruikshank, *Documentary History of the Campaign Upon the Niagara Frontier, Vol. 3* (Welland, ON: The Lundy's Lane Historical Society, 1896–1908), 74.

Chapter 3

1. E.A. Cruikshank, *Documents Relating to the Invasion of Canada and the Surrender of Detroit, Canadian Archives Publications, no. 7* (Ottawa: Government Printing Bureau, 1912), 197.

2. E.A. Cruikshank, *Documentary History of the Campaign Upon The Niagara Frontier*, Major-General Brock to Sir George Prevost, July 28, 1812, 149.

3. *Ibid.*, Brock to Prevost, July 29, 1812, 152–3.

4. *Ibid.*, Brock to Prevost, July 12, 1812, 123.

5. *Ibid.*, Major-General Brock to Noah Freer, York, February 12, 1812, 42.

6. *Ibid.*, Extract of a Letter from ----- to Major-General Van Rensselaer, 16th Sept, 1812, 268.

7. Ferdinand Brock Tupper, *The Life and Correspondence of Major-General Sir Isaac Brock, K.B.* (London: Simpkin, Marshall, 1847), 262.

8. Cruikshank, *Documents Relating to the Invasion*, Brock to Lord Liverpool, 29th August, 1812, 192.

9. Lady Matilda Edgar, *Ten Year of Upper Canada in Peace and War, 1805–1815: Being The Ridout Letters* (Toronto: W. Briggs, 1890), 140.

Chapter 4

1. Cruikshank, *Documentary History, Vol. 3*, 178.

2. *Ibid.*, 213–14, 221.

3. Donald E. Graves, ed., *Merry Hearts Make Light Days: The War of 1812 Memoir of Lieutenant John Le Couteur, 104th Foot* (Ottawa: Carleton University Press, 1993), 135.

4. Cruikshank, *Documentary History Vol. IV*, Narrative of Volunteer G.S. Jarvis, 49th Regiment, 116.

5. Adolphus Egerton Ryerson, *The Loyalists of America and Their Times, Vol. II* (Toronto: W. Briggs, 1880), 370.

6. Cruikshank, *Documentary History, Vol. 4*, 86.

7. *Ibid.*, 83.

8. *Family Herald and Weekly Star*, Author Unknown.

Chapter 5

1. Mary Agnes FitzGibbon, *A Veteran of 1812*, 64.
2. Cruikshank, *Documentary History, Vol. 5*, Sir George Prevost to Lord Bathurst, Kingston, May 26, 1813, 243–44.
3. *Ibid.*, Notes by Captain W.H. Merritt, 262.
4. *Ibid.*, Brigadier-General Vincent to Sir George Prevost, Fort George, May 18, 1813, 237.
5. *Ibid.*, Militia District General Order, Headquarters, Burlington Bay, June 4, 1813, Lieutenant-Colonel J. Harvey, 302.

Chapter 6

1. FitzGibbon, 99.
2. Cruikshank, *Documentary History, Vol. 5*, Brigadier-General Vincent to Colonel Baynes, Bazeley's Head of the Lake, May 31, 1813, 288.
3. Cruikshank, *Documentary History, Vol. 6*, From Lieutenant James FitzGibbon to the Reverend James Somerville of Montreal, 13–15.
4. John K. Green, Grandson of Billy Green, "Billy Green the Scout," *Hamilton Spectator*, 1938.

Chapter 7

1. FitzGibbon, 99.
2. Cruikshank, *Documentary History, Vol. 6*, FitzGibbon to Somerville, 16.
3. FitzGibbon, 72–73.
4. Cruikshank, *Documentary History, Vol. 6*, Lieutenant-Colonel Harvey to Colonel Baynes, Forty Mile Creek, June 11, 1813, 67.
5. FitzGibbon, Appendix VI, James FitzGibbon, "Hints to a Son on Receiving His First Commission in a Regiment Serving in the Canadas."
6. *Ibid.*, Appendix V, *Montreal Gazette*, July 6.

Chapter 8

1. FitzGibbon, 99.

2. Cruikshank, *Documentary History, Vol. 6*, Notes by Captain W.H. Merritt, 123.

3. *Ibid.*, James FitzGibbon to Captain William Kerr, York, March 30, 1818, 120–21.

4. *Ibid.*, Certificate signed by FitzGibbon, Toronto, February 23, 1837, 130.

5. *Ibid.*, Report of a Court of Enquiry on the Conduct of Lieutenant-Colonel Boerstler, Baltimore, February 17, 1815, 153.

Chapter 9

1. Cruikshank, *Documentary History, Vol. 6*, 258.

2. *Ibid.*, *Montreal Gazette*, July 6, 1813, 116.

3. FitzGibbon, Appendix V1.

4. *Ibid.*, 109.

5. *Ibid.*, 111.

6. Cruikshank, *Documentary History Vol. 6*, Major-General De Rottenburg to Sir George Prevost, 12 Mile Creek, July 7, 1813, 199.

7. *Ibid.*, Notes by Captain W.H. Merritt, 174.

8. *Ibid.*, Major-General De Rottenburg to Sir George Prevost, July 20, 1813, 253–54.

9. Cruikshank, *Documentary History, Vol. 3*, Sir George Prevost to Sir James Lucas Yeo, Kingston, September 19, 1813, 148–49.

10. Dr. William Dunlop, *Recollections of the War of 1812* (Toronto: Historical Publishing Co., 1908), 55.

11. Lady Matilda Edgar, *Ten Years of Upper Canada in Peace and War*, 212, 225, 227.

Chapter 10

1. Lady Matilda Edgar, *Ten Years of Upper Canada in Peace and War*, 266.

2. William H. Wood, ed., *Select British Documents of the Canadian War of 1812, Vol. 2* (Toronto: Chaplain Society, 1920–28), Barclay to Yeo, September 6, 1813, 292.

3. Lady Matilda Edgar, 228.
4. *Ibid.*, 231.
5. Cruikshank, *Documentary History, Vol. 8*, 59.
6. Lady Matilda Edgar, 238–39.

Chapter 11

1. Cruikshank, *Documentary History, Vol. 8*, 177.
2. Cruikshank, *Documentary History, Vol. 4*, Extract of a letter from an Officer in the Army, dated Grenadier Island, October 26, 1813, 95.
3. *Ibid.*, Major-General Wilkinson to the Secretary of War, Grenadier Island, November 1, 1813, 121.
4. Lady Matilda Edgar, 243–44.
5. Cruikshank, *Documentary History, Vol. 4*, From Major-General Wilkinson to Major-General Hampton, 7 miles above Ogdensburg, November 6, 1813, 140.
6. Lady Matilda Edgar, Thomas G. Ridout to father, Prescott, November 9, 1813, 251.
7. *Ibid.*, Ridout to father, Montreal, November 20, 1813, 256.
8. Cruikshank, *Documentary History, Vol. 8*, Memorandum of the Services of Lieutenant-Colonel Charles Plenderleath, January 1, 1854, by Colonel James FitzGibbon, 165.
9. Croil, 78.

Chapter 12

1. Cruikshank, *Documentary History, Vol. 1*, 114–15.
2. Cruikshank, *Documentary History, Vol. 9*, From the *National Advocate*, New York, December 31, 1813, 40.
3. *Ibid.*, From Sir George Prevost to Lieutenant General Drummond, Montreal, April 30, 1814, 319.
4. Cruikshank, *Documentary History, Vol. 1*, Sir Gordon Drummond to Sir George Prevost, Niagara Falls, July 27, 1814, 85–86.

5. *Ibid.*, General Brown to Commodore Chauncey, Queenston, July 13, 1814, 64.
6. *Ibid.*, Major MacFarland, 23rd U.S. Infantry, to his wife, 73.

Chapter 13

1. Cruikshank, *Documentary History, Vol. 1*, 105.
2. *Ibid.*, Dr. Bull to ----, Buffalo, July 31, 1814, 104.
3. *Ibid.*, Sir G. Drummond to Sir George Prevost, Niagara Falls, July 27, 1814, 91, 117.
4. *Ibid.*, Lieutenant-General Drummond to Sir George Prevost, Camp Before Fort Erie, August 12, 1814, 133.
5. Dr. William Dunlop, *Recollections of the War of 1812*, 67–69.
6. *Ibid.*, 73.
7. Anna Jameson, 59.
8. Cruikshank, *Documentary History, Vol. 1*, Sir George Prevost to Vice-Admiral the Honourable Alexander Cochrane, Montreal, July 30, 1814, 177.

Chapter 14

1. Cruikshank, *Documentary History, Vol. 2*, 290.
2. Cruikshank, *Documentary History, Vol. 1*, Sir G. Drummond to Sir J. Yeo, Camp Before Fort Erie, 182, 185.
3. Dr. William Dunlop, *Recollections of the War of 1812*, 58–59.
4. Cruikshank, *Documentary History, Vol. 1*, Major-General De Watteville to Sir Gordon Drummond, Camp Before Fort Erie, September 19, 1814, 204.
5. Cruikshank, *Documentary History, Vol. 1*, Lieutenant-General Drummond to Sir George Prevost, Camp Before Fort Erie, September 19, 1814, 205.
6. *Ibid.*, Sir Gordon Drummond to Sir George Prevost, October 11 and 15, 1814, 250, 253.
7. *Ibid.*, Lieutenant-Colonel Christopher Myers, October 19, 1814, 261.
8. FitzGibbon, Appendix XIII.

Chapter 15

1. FitzGibbon, Appendix XIII.
2. *Ibid.*, 158–59.
3. Anna Jameson, 60–61.
4. FitzGibbon, 202–03.
5. *Ibid.*, Appendix VIII.
6. *Ibid.*, 226–27.
7. *Ibid.*, 256.
8. *Ibid.*, 258–59.
9. *Ibid.*, 313.

BIBLIOGRAPHY

Berton, Pierre. *Flames Across the Border: 1813–1814*. Toronto: McClelland & Stewart, 1981.

___. *The Invasion of Canada: 1812–1813*. Toronto: McClelland & Stewart, 1980.

Cruikshank, E.A. *Documentary History of the Campaign Upon The Niagara Frontier, Part 3*. Welland, ON: The Lundy's Lane Historical Society, 1896–1908.

___. *Documents Relating to the Invasion of Canada and the Surrender of Detroit, Canadian Archives Publications, no. 7*. Ottawa: Government Printing Bureau, 1912.

Dunlop, William. *Recollections of the War of 1812*. Toronto: Historical Publishing Co., 1908.

Edgar, Lady Matilda. *Ten Years of Upper Canada in Peace and War, 1805–1815: Being the Ridout Letters*. Toronto: W. Briggs, 1890.

FitzGibbon, Mary Agnes. *A Veteran of 1812: The Life of James FitzGibbon*. Toronto, William Briggs, 1894.

Graves, Donald E. *Field of Glory, The Battle of Crysler's Farm, 1813*. Toronto: Robin Brass Studio, 1999.

___. *Merry Hearts Make Light Days, War of 1812 Memoirs of Lieutenant John Le Couteur, 104th Foot*. Ottawa: Carleton University Press, 1993.

Guillet, Edwin. *Pioneer Settlements*. Toronto: The Ontario Publishing Co., 1947.

___. *Pioneer Travel*. Toronto: The Ontario Publishing Co., 1939.

Hitsman, J. Mackay. *The Incredible War of 1812: A Military History.* Toronto: University of Toronto Press, 1966.

Jeffreys, C.W. *The Picture Gallery of Canadian History, Vols. 2 and 3.* Toronto: The Ryerson Press, 1945 and 1950.

Lossing, Benson. *Pictorial Field Book of the War of 1812.* New York: Harper & Brothers, 1869.

McKenzie, Ruth. *Leeds and Grenville: Their First Two Hundred Years.* Toronto: McClelland & Stewart, 1967.

Read, David B. *Life and Times of Major-General Sir Isaac Brock, K.B.* Toronto: W. Briggs, 1894.

Ryerson, Adolphus Edgerton. *The Loyalists of America and Their Times.* Toronto: Briggs, 1880.

Tupper, Ferdinand Brock. *The Life and Correspondence of Major-General Sir Isaac Brock, K.B.* London: Simpkin, Marshall, 1847.

Way, Ronald E. *The Day of Crysler's Farm.* Morrisburg, ON: The Ontario-St. Lawrence Development Commission.

INDEX

MORE GREAT DUNDURN TITLES FOR YOUNG ADULTS

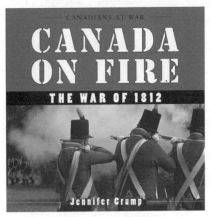

Canada on Fire
The War of 1812
Jennifer Crump
978-1-554887538 / $19.99

The summer of 1812 saw the beginning of one of the most brutal wars to take place on Canadian soil. With more than 1,600 people killed and a battlefront that extended from Halifax Harbour in Nova Scotia to the Columbia River in what is now British Columbia, the war featured many brave men and women who fended off much larger American forces.

Canada on Fire is an exciting account of the War of 1812 as told through the stories of the heroes who helped to defend Canada, people such as Mohawk chief John Norton, who led a small army into battle against the wishes of his tribe, and Red George Macdonnell, who spent the war defending the St. Lawrence River.

With descriptions of the battle at Lundy's Lane, the adventures of the Sea Wolves, and the antics of James FitzGibbon and his Bloody Boys, *Canada on Fire* reveals the War of 1812 as it has seldom been seen.

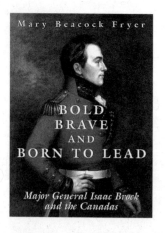

Bold, Brave, and Born to Lead
Major General Isaac Brock and the Canadas
Mary Beacock Fryer
978-1-550025019
$12.99

Celebrated as the saviour of Upper Canada, Major-General Sir Isaac Brock was a charismatic leader who won the respect not only of his own troops, but also of the Shawnee chief Tecumseh and even men among his enemy. His motto could well have been "speak loud and look big." Although this attitude earned him a reputation for brashness, it also enabled his success and propelled him into the significant role he would play in the War of 1812.

Available at your favourite bookseller.

www.dundurn.com

What did you think of this book?
Visit www.dundurn.com for reviews, videos, updates, and more!

RECYCLED
Paper made from
recycled material
FSC® C103567

Marquis Book Printing Inc.

Québec, Canada
2011

Printed on Silva Enviro 100% post-consumer EcoLogo certified paper,
processed chlorine free and manufactured using biogas energy.